Living and Dying in Joy

Living and Dying in Joy

A Devotional Guide
to the Heidelberg Catechism

Cornelis Vonk

Translated by
Nelson D. Kloosterman

Edited by
Jordan J. Ballor

GRAND RAPIDS · MICHIGAN

PAIDEIA
PRESS

© 2013 Christian's Library Press
An imprint of the Acton Institute for the Study of Religion & Liberty
98 East Fulton   Phone: 616.454.3080
Grand Rapids, Michigan 49503   Fax: 616.454.9454
www.clpress.com

Copublished with Paideia Press
Grand Rapids, Michigan, 49507
thereformationalpublishingproject.com

ISBN: 978-1-93894869-5

Scripture quotations not referenced by chapter and verse are translated from the author's Dutch translation or paraphrase.

Unless otherwise indicated, Scripture quotations referenced by chapter and verse are from the ESV® Bible (The Holy Bible, English Standard Version®) copyright © 2001 by Crossway, a publishing ministry of Good News Publishers. Used by permission. All rights reserved.

Cover image: "Lazarus and the Rich Man" by Eduard von Gebhardt, 1865, public domain.

Cover design by Peter Ho
Editorial assistance by Dylan Pahman and Joe Carter

Printed in the United States of America

1 2 3 4 5 6   18 17 16 15 14 13

Contents

FOREWORD

Every Sunday for forty years, from 1932 until 1973, the Rev. Cornelis Vonk preached the Word of God in Schiedam, the Netherlands, as a Reformed minister. I can still see him in his black robe ascending the pulpit with dignity, always with the Bible under his arm.

He was even more clear and stimulating as a teacher of Holy Scripture on the pulpit than he was with the pen. Sunday mornings he would often preach through a book of the Bible in series. His sermons were always arranged in terms of the basics of exegesis: pay attention to the text, the context, and the canonical place (or perhaps in reverse order). Anyone shaped by his preaching would later be surprised when preachers treated a text without first examining its larger context, for they had become accustomed to Vonk's approach. The other approach they would call "hobbyhorse preaching."

During all those years, Vonk provided the congregation on Sunday afternoons with scriptural teaching using the Heidelberg Catechism. He always began his catechism sermons with the following sentence: "Congregation, I open God's Word to you according to what we confess about it in Lord's Day" such-and-such. This is how he let us know that he was not preaching on the Catechism, but just as he had done in the morning, he was opening God's Word, except this time concerning a subject that was being treated in that Lord's Day.

He stuck to that opening sentence. In his catechism sermons, he did not regale the congregation with morsels of theology and watered-down systematic theology, but supplied fully biblical instruction. On Sunday mornings he stuck with the announced text or passage, but on Sunday afternoons he walked freely from Moses to Paul and from the Psalms to the Prophets. He was always keenly aware that he stood before God's baptized covenant congregation. He would often weave into his afternoon sermons interesting lessons drawn from church history.

Vonk had a good voice. He always began his sermons and addresses slowly and solemnly, and he would gradually increase his tempo. He always had in front of him his sermon, written out fully in pen. He never learned to type. He talked in ordinary Dutch, even when this was not yet the universal custom. He often used rhetorical questions like "What do you suppose?," "Don't you agree?," "Do you remember?," "Have you ever . . . ?," and the like.

In 1950 Vonk's extensive 700-page commentary on the Heidelberg Catechism and on the liturgical Form for Baptism appeared as part of the series The Aforesaid Doctrine (*De Voorzeide Leer*). The volumes of this series focusing on the biblical books are now appearing in English translation as Opening the Scriptures. This commentary was the compilation of his preaching and catechizing throughout the years. The book was intended for catechism students, but many a minister made grateful use of it for his own catechism sermons. It is not a theological work, but it shows with abundant clarity that the Catechism is a genuine confessional document that echoes Scripture. For to confess is to say the same thing that Scripture says. By far the greatest effort was devoted to including references to Scripture.

The same is true of the book you are now reading. This is a revised and abbreviated edition of the extensive explanation that Vonk himself wrote with his own hand. This smaller volume shows with special clarity that what the church confesses in the Heidelberger has been drawn thoroughly from Scripture and is according to Scripture. It will certainly be able to serve as a brief introduction to Christian doctrine, for example, for those desiring to become members of the church.

People can use this little volume in other ways, however. Because it contains many cited Scripture references, a family with growing children can read through this book for mealtime devotions in the span of seven weeks. I recall an elderly Christian woman who sought her comfort every evening by reading a "Lord's Day" from the Catechism as she lay for an extended time on her deathbed. Why couldn't a pastor read a Catechism Lord's Day to someone on their sickbed, if possible with a brief explanation along with it? Is not the phrase "book of comfort" a subtitle for the Catechism?

How did Rev. Vonk teach his catechism students in his weekly catechism classes? In the way that was customary at the time: by talking in a friendly atmosphere in a way that was as stimulating as possible, telling what God has done for us and promised to us through the Lord Jesus. We had to memorize only Lord's Days 1, 7, and 23. The long answer to question 74, "Should infants, too, be baptized?," we did not need to learn entirely by memory, as long as we remembered the word *Yes!* He said this "*Yes!*" so loudly that many a former catechism student, including the undersigned, remembers it still in his old age.

May the remembrance of this righteous saint be a blessing, also through this posthumous publication (Prov. 10:7).

The Rev. Frans van Deursen
Barneveld, The Netherlands

TRANSLATOR'S PREFACE

The occasion for the appearance of this modest commentary is the 450th anniversary of the publication of the Heidelberg Catechism in 1563. As one of the most beloved catechisms produced in the time of the Reformation, the Heidelberger has been a rich source of comfort, instruction, and witness.

Several matters of note relating to the translation will aid the reader. Unless otherwise noted, the version of the English Bible cited is the English Standard Version (ESV). The version of the English translation of the Heidelberg Catechism is the one produced by the Canadian Reformed Churches, revised at points in terms of American spelling conventions, contemporary grammatical usage, and the use of the ESV.

This translation was made from a handwritten manuscript penned by Rev. Vonk in the closing years of his life. We thank the Rev. Frans van Deursen for his invaluable assistance in helping to decipher Rev. Vonk's penmanship and to explain the text at points.

We express our deep gratitude to Mr. John Hultink for the financial sponsorship of this translation. John's commitment to the Christian faith, specifically to that expression of the faith known as Calvinism, has throughout the years been both intense and sacrificial. With this volume we honor that commitment.

For those able to read the Dutch language, Rev. Vonk's more elaborate commentary appearing in *De Voorzeide Leer* (The Aforesaid Doctrine), provides more extensive discussions drawn from his many years of fruitful preaching and pastoring. With the publication of this abridgment comes the prayer that the Lord will bless his people with fresh devotion to him and his ways.

Nelson D. Kloosterman
January 19, 2013
Saint John, Indiana, USA

LORD'S DAY I

Introduction

The term *catechism* refers to a book that teaches by means of questions and answers. In the sixteenth century, when the church was being reformed, such catechisms were authored especially for instructing the church's youth. During that time, a variety of faithful pastors of the church provided such a primer for the children. Ours has come from Heidelberg. This was the capital city of the royal territory of the Palatinate. Because this catechism corresponded so well with Holy Scripture, it was accepted in the Netherlands as an expression of the Christian faith. It was also stipulated as a standard for the preaching of the Word, and for that reason it was divided into fifty-two Lord's Days. Each Sunday the minister of the Word was supposed to explain a portion of the Heidelberg Catechism by means of instruction from God's Word. For that is the key of salvation (Luke 11:52; Rom. 10:14, 17; 2 Tim. 3:15–16). Parents must acquaint their children with the Word from their youth. Moses commanded that back in Deuteronomy 4:9. Paul did as well, in Ephesians 6:4. Therefore the complete title of the Heidelberg Catechism was *Catechism or instruction in the Christian doctrine that is taught in the Reformed churches and schools in the Netherlands*.

The man who ordered the writing of the Catechism was the prince of the Palatinate, Frederick III. His doctrinal manual was published in 1563 thanks to the labors of various scholars. The Heidelberg Catechism immediately came under attack; Frederick defended it, however, even when he had to appear before the imperial court, just as Luther had done almost a half century earlier. With Paul, he confessed, "But the Lord stood by me and strengthened me, so that through me the message might be fully proclaimed and all the Gentiles might hear it. So I was rescued from the lion's mouth" (2 Tim. 4:17). We must specifically not underestimate that evil power. Prince Frederick spoke about that in Question and Answer 1 of the Catechism.

Q&A 1

Q. *What is your only comfort in life and death?*

A. That I am not my own, but belong with body and soul, both in life and in death, to my faithful Savior Jesus Christ. He has fully paid for all my sins with his precious blood, and has set me free from all the power of the devil. He also preserves me in such a way that without the will of my heavenly Father not a hair can fall from my head; indeed, all things must work together for my salvation. Therefore, by his Holy Spirit he also assures me of eternal life and makes me heartily willing and ready from now on to live for him.

Here God's church confesses something, first, about the Lord Jesus; next, about the Father of our Lord Jesus; and third, about the Holy Spirit.

The Lord Jesus came to earth to destroy the works of the devil (1 John 3:8). Paul was called to be an apostle in order to save pagans from the power of Satan (Acts 26:18). Christ himself once spoke of the kingdom of Satan (Matt. 12:26). And Paul once called Satan "the god of this world" (2 Cor. 4:4). Even today many pagans do not know Jesus and thus do not honor him, just like many of our pagan ancestors. Satan will be defeated definitively only when Jesus returns one day, but our Savior has already shed his blood for us on the cross (1 Cor. 6:20) and already now is crowned in heaven with honor and glory (Heb. 2:9). Whoever believes in him belongs to Jesus and is his possession now and for all eternity (John 10:28–29). Those who believe in Jesus belong to him for their entire lives, including when they have died and lie somewhere in the bosom of the earth, for at his return Jesus will raise them.

The Father of our Savior loves all who love his Son, and he will care for them so that no one harms even one hair (Matt. 10:29–31). Our heavenly Father can turn adversity to our good (Rom. 8:28). Now that our Lord Jesus has provided us such a Father, we can travel our pathway with peace of mind.

The Holy Spirit provides that peace and comfort. Even though many of our ancestors were formerly pagans, they were brought by the Holy Spirit into the light of the gospel of Christ. Thanks to that light we too may see that we no longer stand under the power of Satan, but belong to the property of Christ. He paid for us with the incalculably high cost of his blood. By means of the gospel of such a Father who handed his Son over for our sake, the Holy Spirit impels us to genuine, ordinary Christian faith and life.

Q&A 2

Q. *What do you need to know in order to live and die in the joy of this comfort?*

A. First, how great my sins and misery are; second, how I am delivered from all my sins and misery; third, how I am to be thankful to God for such deliverance.

What a beautifully clear overview! Three parts: misery, redemption, and gratitude. However, you should be warned. These parts are chapters, chapters of the teaching manual. Most importantly, they are not to be understood as stages or as sequential phases of our life. There is not first a phase of sinful living, followed by the beginning stage of redemption, with everything concluding at that point with the phase of gratitude.

That is thoroughly mistaken!

These are not three parts of our life. We make this claim, first, because our misery, namely, that we are inclined to sin and depravity, lasts our entire life. Second, our redemption also lasts our entire life, for until death we continue to need forgiveness through Christ's blood, together with undergoing the dying of our old nature and the coming to life of our new nature. Third, our gratitude for God's salvation must also be shown throughout our entire lifetime, for the Lord has already granted his salvation in his covenant promise and sealed it with his baptism.

Scripture References

Matthew 10:29–31
"Are not two sparrows sold for a penny? And not one of them will fall to the ground apart from your Father. But even the hairs of your head are all numbered. Fear not, therefore; you are of more value than many sparrows."

Luke 11:52
"Woe to you lawyers! For you have taken away the key of knowledge. You did not enter yourselves, and you hindered those who were entering."

Luke 12:22–34
And he said to his disciples, "Therefore I tell you, do not be anxious about your life, what you will eat, nor about your body, what you will put on. For life is more than food, and the body more than clothing. Consider the ravens: they neither sow nor reap, they have neither storehouse nor barn, and yet God feeds them. Of how much more value are you than the birds! And which of you by being anxious can add a single hour to his span of life? If then you are not able to do as small a thing as that, why are you anxious about the rest? Consider the lilies, how they grow: they neither toil nor spin, yet I tell you, even Solomon in all his glory was not arrayed like one of these. But if God so clothes the grass, which is alive in the field today, and tomorrow is thrown into the oven, how much more will he clothe you, O you of little faith! And do not seek what you are to eat and what you are to drink, nor be worried. For all the nations of the world seek after these things, and your Father knows that you need them. Instead, seek his kingdom, and these things will be added to you.

"Fear not, little flock, for it is your Father's good pleasure to give you the kingdom. Sell your possessions, and give to the needy. Provide yourselves with moneybags that do not grow old, with a treasure in the heavens that does not fail, where no thief approaches and no moth destroys. For where your treasure is, there will your heart be also."

John 6:39
"And this is the will of him who sent me, that I should lose nothing of all that he has given me, but raise it up on the last day."

Romans 10:14
How then will they call on him in whom they have not believed? And how are they to believe in him of whom they have never heard? And how are they to hear without someone preaching?

Romans 10:17
So faith comes from hearing, and hearing through the word of Christ.

Ephesians 1:13–14
In him you also, when you heard the word of truth, the gospel of your salvation, and believed in him, were sealed with the promised Holy Spirit, who is the guarantee of our inheritance until we acquire possession of it, to the praise of his glory.

Ephesians 6:4
Fathers, do not provoke your children to anger, but bring them up in the discipline and instruction of the Lord.

2 Timothy 3:16–17
All Scripture is breathed out by God and profitable for teaching, for reproof, for correction, and for training in righteousness, that the man of God may be complete, equipped for every good work.

LORD'S DAY 2

Here begins the first section of our manual. This section deals with our misery, or with the knowledge of our sin, specifically with guilt for sin (Lord's Day 3), and the punishment for sin (Lord's Day 4).

Q&A 3

Q. *From where do you know your sins and misery?*

A. From the law of God.

No one reaches this knowledge by himself, namely, the acknowledgment that we are people who are filled with sins and blemishes. One can see this clearly with pagans and the unconverted. Rather than being ashamed of their sins, they boast in their sins instead, as Lamech did, for example, when he said, "I have killed a man for wounding me, a young man for striking me" (Gen. 4:23), and as the Pharisee did when he praised himself in the parable (Luke 18:11–12). Little wonder. In the darkness one sees little, but through the light of God's Word we can observe our depravity. For through his Word God acquaints us with his law as the rule that must direct our heart and life. Adam knew very well what behavior God desired from him, for he had walked with God in the garden (Gen. 3:8). Too bad that what he told his descendants about God did not remain known to most of them. For pagans have suppressed the truth in unrighteousness, so that their heart is darkened (Rom. 1:18, 21). But Abraham, Isaac, and Jacob received God's Word once again and kept it (Gen. 26:5). Israel could sing that God had made known to her his statutes and ordinances, as he had done to no other people (Ps. 147:19–20). Israel received God's Word through Moses and other prophets (Rom. 2:17–18; 3:2; 9:4). Thereby she could clearly know God's covenant and commandments. But among pagans some knowledge of good and evil lived in their heart by means of being passed down through the generations (Rom. 2:15; sometimes in Scripture the heart refers to memory; see Luke 2:51). Because of this voice of conscience, many pagans have had difficulty with the self-condemnation that conscience might bring. But when many Jews in his day no longer understood God's Word and commandment, Paul wrote that they indeed possessed the law but had rendered it powerless (Rom. 8:3).

In Scripture the term *law* sometimes indicates the entire Word of God given at that time, what we today call the Old Testament (Pss. 19; 119; John 10:34). Sometimes the term *law* is applied to the five books of Moses (Matt. 5:17; Luke 24:44; John 1:45). At other times it refers to the shadowy gospel or the visual instruction by means of blood, sacrifices, altars, and priests (Heb. 10:1; Gal. 3:24).

That shadowy gospel is the same one that we are privileged to know (see the Belgic Confession, art. 25). This teaches us that just like Israel, the covenant people of old, we too must be purified daily from our sins through Christ's atoning blood (1 John 1:7), and that the Lord Jesus prays for us continually (Heb. 7:25).

God gave the law to his people Israel for their life (Rom. 7:10). But rather than letting themselves be led humbly by God's law, many, like the Pharisees, dared to exalt themselves above the law. This rendered the law powerless. They nonetheless looked down their noses at the Gentiles, for the Gentiles did not know the law. God, however, had intended that through his lovely law, Israel would expect everything from his grace. Paul frequently called that a wanting to live apart "from the law" (Rom. 7:9), and he condemned such self-directed piety as belonging to "the flesh" (Rom. 7:14).

No, the truth is that nobody can obtain the salvation they

need from "the works of the law" (that is, by means of a self-directed religious life like that of the Pharisees). On the contrary, they thereby render themselves even more guilty than the Gentiles. For the taller one stands, the harder one falls. From the law, the Pharisees should have understood that they were sinners, and they should have been driven to God's grace, for no one can keep God's commandments perfectly (1 Kgs. 8:46; Jas. 2:10; 3:2). Therefore, they should not have turned the law into a rule that we simply need to keep and on which we can then rely. Instead of our obedience being perfect, our sins are so great that the law curses us (Gal. 3:10; Col. 2:14). This "curse of the law" can be removed by none other than our Lord Jesus Christ (Gal. 3:13).

Q&A 4

Q. *What does God's law require of us?*

A. Christ teaches us this in a summary in Matthew 22: You shall love the Lord your God with all your heart and with all your soul and with all your mind. This is the great and first commandment. And a second is like it: You shall love your neighbor as yourself. On these two commandments depend all the Law and the Prophets.

When we use the word *law*, we must not think exclusively of the Ten Commandments. With the word *law*, Scripture can refer to far more, namely, to the entire Word of God. The Hebrew word for "law" (*torah*) means "instruction, insight, teaching." In the Ten Commandments, God gave Israel the rules of the covenant. Israel was called to live according to them as God's covenant people (Exod. 20). We read frequently about "the words of the covenant" (Exod. 34:28). The two stones on which God wrote with his own finger were called "the two tablets of stone, the tablets of the covenant" (Deut. 9:11).

There was once a teacher of the law who wanted to give the Lord Jesus an examination, as it were (Matt. 22:34–40). The rabbis had devised long lists of more than 600 prescriptions and prohibitions. They divided these into lighter and heavier commands. They reasoned like this: God is greater than a human being; so then, if your parents have become so poor that you must help them with money, but you give that money instead to the temple of God, then the latter is more commendable, even if your parents must suffer greater deprivation (Mark 7:10–13).

One day that teacher of the law asked the Lord Jesus which command of those hundreds was the most important.

Jesus never addressed that issue, but summarized God's entire law in two commandments. He quoted the first from Deuteronomy 6:5, which taught that the Israelites must love God with their whole *heart* (the center from which a person does everything), with their entire *soul* (a word used often for a person's desire and craving), with their whole *mind*, and with all their *strength* (in our arms and legs). To show that naturally no competition could exist among God's commandments, Jesus followed with his second quotation, from Leviticus 19:18: "You shall love your neighbor as yourself." The Savior said at the same time that these two commands summarized everything God desired for Israel's life-conduct as he had revealed in the Bible (simply the Old Testament, namely, the books of Moses, the Prophets, and the Writings). Love God and love one's neighbor. The apostle Paul later wrote that love is the fulfillment of the law (Rom. 13:10).

Q&A 5

Q. *Can you keep all this perfectly?*

A. No, I am inclined by nature to hate God and my neighbor.

Scripture teaches that believers love God's commandments (see Ps. 119:47). Paul wrote in Romans 7:22, "For I delight in the law of God, in my inner being," that is to say, in my heart. When we live by the Spirit of Christ, the righteousness of the law is once again fulfilled in us (Rom. 8:4). But in no sense are believers perfect in this keeping of the law, as the Bible's history teaches us: Noah (drunkenness), Abraham (lying), Jacob (deceit), David (adultery and murder), and Peter (denial).

This is what 1 John 1:8 teaches as well. Such sins are due to the weaknesses of our flesh; *flesh* is a word that occasionally refers to depraved human nature. See, for example, Romans 7:18: "For I know that nothing good dwells in me, that is, in my flesh." And again, see Romans 8:7: "For the mind that is set on the flesh is hostile to God." Other phrases for this are "what is earthly in you" (Col. 3:5), "the old self" (Col. 3:9; Rom. 6:6), the sin that dwells in us (Rom. 7:17, 20). Even though our heart has been moved to serve God once again, the inclination to fall back into evil remains with us our whole life. Paul complained with sadness, "For I do not understand my own actions. For I do not do what I want, but I do the very thing I hate" (Rom. 7:15).

Precisely because of this, believers are not impressed with themselves, as were the Pharisees, who through their self-directed interpretation had disfigured God's commandments into a system of human statutes (Matt. 15:6; Mark 7:13). Their self-invented teaching lay like a veil over their face, so that they could no longer read God's actual Word when they read Moses and the Prophets (2 Cor. 3:15). They felt free to murder God's Son, who alone sounded forth the simple word of God (John 11:47–50). Let us pray to God that our old nature may never obtain so much power over us. For example, by nature we are inclined to repay someone who has hit us with a slap in return, but God does not want that. Love is not resentful (1 Cor. 13:5).

Scripture References

Romans 7:18
For I know that nothing good dwells in me, that is, in my flesh. For I have the desire to do what is right, but not the ability to carry it out.

Romans 8:6–7
For to set the mind on the flesh is death, but to set the mind on the Spirit is life and peace. For the mind that is set on the flesh is hostile to God, for it does not submit to God's law; indeed, it cannot.

2 Corinthians 7:1–10

Since we have these promises, beloved, let us cleanse ourselves from every defilement of body and spirit, bringing holiness to completion in the fear of God.

Make room in your hearts for us. We have wronged no one, we have corrupted no one, we have taken advantage of no one. I do not say this to condemn you, for I said before that you are in our hearts, to die together and to live together. I am acting with great boldness toward you; I have great pride in you; I am filled with comfort. In all our affliction, I am over-flowing with joy.

For even when we came into Macedonia, our bodies had no rest, but we were afflicted at every turn—fighting without and fear within. But God, who comforts the downcast, comforted us by the coming of Titus, and not only by his coming but also by the comfort with which he was comforted by you, as he told us of your longing, your mourning, your zeal for me, so that I rejoiced still more. For even if I made you grieve with my letter, I do not regret it—though I did regret it, for I see that that letter grieved you, though only for a while. As it is, I rejoice, not because you were grieved, but because you were grieved into repenting. For you felt a godly grief, so that you suffered no loss through us. For godly grief produces a repen-tance that leads to salvation without regret, whereas worldly grief pro-duces death.

Lord's Day 3

Q&A 6

Q. *Did God, then, create man so wicked and perverse?*

A. No, on the contrary, God created man good and in his image, that is, in true righteousness and holiness, so that he might rightly know God his Creator, heartily love him, and live with him in eternal blessedness to praise and glorify him.

The question is obvious: How did we get this way? God did not create us this way, did he?

We hardly get started reading Scripture in Genesis 1 when we read, "And God saw everything that he had made, and behold, it was very good" (Gen. 1:31). Indeed, we even read that God created man "in his own image" (Gen. 1:27). This does not mean that man was or could become partially like God. But it does mean that we could believe in God and obey his will. Unfortunately, people no longer can do this perfectly. There was only One who perfectly fulfilled God's mandate: Jesus! God's plan is that one day we will share with Christ in that glory on the new earth, and then we will be conformed to God's Son. Christ will be the Firstborn (the Eldest) among many brothers (Rom. 8:29). But we are not there yet. That is still coming (1 Cor. 15:49; 1 John 3:2). Using a metaphor of removing and putting on a garment, the apostle commands us to put away the old nature and to put on the new nature that is being renewed in the image of its Creator (Col. 3:10).

Just as a good son is occasionally identified with his father, and as the conduct of a governing official occasionally shows forth something of the majesty of his prince, so too Adam was created in God's image. The appearance of pagans who came to believe in Christ changed to such an extent that Paul wrote to the Ephesians, "But that is not the way you learned Christ!—assuming that you have heard about him and were taught in him, as the truth is in Jesus, to put off your old self, which belongs to your former manner of life and is corrupt through deceitful desires, and to be renewed in the spirit of your minds, and to put on the new self, created after the likeness of God in true righteousness and holiness" (Eph. 4:20–24). By becoming Christians they were no longer slaves of sin, but had acquired a royal dimension. Formerly they had been rebellious against God's will, but now they had been recreated in God's image, "in true righteousness and holiness."

We may also render this phrase as "in true justification and holiness." These two words appear frequently in Holy Scripture.

The righteous person is the opposite of the wicked person (Gen. 18:23; Ps. 37:16; Prov. 24:24). In Psalm 112 such a righteous person is described as someone who takes great delight in God's commands and who hates sin (see Prov. 12:3; 13:5). The righteousness of the godly refers to their walk in the fear of the Lord, their obedience to and keeping of God's Word and command (Gen. 18:19; Ps. 15:2; Luke 1:6; 2:25).

The word *holy* (and the verb *to sanctify*) is used especially in a twofold sense. First, it means being separated from the world and set apart for the service of God. This meaning is hardly restricted to people, for Scripture also talks about pots and pans being "holy" (Exod. 40:9–15). The entire tribe of Levi was "holy" as well, that is, separated for the service of the sanctuary. The people of Israel were "holy" in the sense that they were not permitted to engage in pagan practices (Deut. 14:1). God had sanctified the Israelites for himself by their baptism in the Red Sea (1 Cor. 10:1–4). By virtue of the covenant promise the children of the church are also "holy" and have the right to be baptized (1 Cor. 7:14).

But the word *holy* can also be used in reference to a person's heart and walk: "Strive for peace with everyone, and for the holiness without which no one will see the Lord" (Heb. 12:14; see also 1 Pet. 1:15; 2 Cor. 7:1).

These two meanings of *holy* must not be confused. For example, the children of the church are indeed recognized as members of the church, by virtue of the promise of the covenant in which God has granted them the washing away of sins through Christ's blood and renewing through his Spirit. But just as many Israelites who died in the wilderness on account of their unbelief did not receive the promised land (Num. 20:12; Heb. 4:2), so too there are church members who have trampled underfoot the gospel of Christ and his blood with which they were sanctified (Heb. 10:29; 12:16).

The word *holy* applies to all church members in terms of its first meaning, but not in terms of its second meaning.

Q&A 7

Q. *From where, then, did man's depraved nature come?*

A. From the fall and disobedience of our first parents, Adam and Eve, in Paradise, for there our nature became so corrupt that we are all conceived and born in sin.

As they are growing up, boys and girls sometimes disobey a command of their parents. For example, when father says, "Tonight you must be home by ten o'clock!" then one of them might say, "We will see." This "seeing" actually signifies an overthrowing of the parental directive.

When God created man, man was initially good and obedient. But that changed drastically.

Two trees stood in the center of Paradise. God gave each tree a name. The one came to be called "the tree of life," and the other, "the tree of the knowledge of good and evil."

We must look at the second tree first. Concerning this tree, God had said that the man was permitted to eat from every tree in the garden except from the tree of the knowledge of good and evil. Would the man want to "see" for himself what good and evil were, or would he acknowledge that what God had prohibited was indeed dangerous? Sadly, the man listened to the devil. The devil used the serpent to tempt the man to a fatal fall (John 8:44). He lied to the man, telling him that he could "see" for himself—that he could determine for himself—what was good and evil. The man listened to the devil, and the consequences were terrible. God was so merciful as to spare Adam's life. Adam lived until he was 930 years old, and together with his wife, Eve, he produced sons and daughters, from whom we have descended. The children grew up and demonstrated that what issued from their heart was also evil. Whatever is "born of the flesh is flesh," Jesus said (John 3:6; see Ps. 51:7; Job 14:4).

Q&A 8

Q. *But are we so corrupt that we are totally unable to do any good and inclined to all evil?*

A. Yes, unless we are regenerated by the Spirit of God.

Those words at the end of the preceding paragraph (whatever is "born of the flesh is flesh") were spoken by the Lord Jesus to Nicodemus, a Pharisee. The Pharisees thought their righteousness was very great (see our discussion of Q&A 6). In reality they were disobedient to God. They had buried God's Word so deeply under their self-invented doctrine that they did not recognize God's Word in the preaching of John the Baptist and refused to submit to it (Luke 7:30). They did the same with the preaching of the Lord Jesus (John 3:11). Only a person who obeys God's straightforward Word is spiritual. For it pleases the Holy Spirit to incline our hearts through the Word to true faith and, in doing so, to lead us to live a God-fearing life. Through faith he regenerates us and makes us new people (Belgic Confession, art. 22–24), who once again display the image of God through true righteousness and holiness.

What a sorrowful review that was. The man, created so beautifully, through his own disobedience became incapable of any good and inclined to all evil. His children after him were the same. If God had not given his Spirit to our ancestors, we would not have been born and raised as Christian children, but would have been like the pagans. Paul confessed: our sufficiency is God's work (2 Cor. 3:5).

Scripture References

Genesis 1:27

> So God created man in his own image,
>> in the image of God he created him;
>> male and female he created them.

Genesis 2:16–17

And the Lord God commanded the man, saying, "You may surely eat of every tree of the garden, but of the tree of the knowledge of good and evil you shall not eat, for in the day that you eat of it you shall surely die."

John 3:3

Jesus answered him, "Truly, truly, I say to you, unless one is born again he cannot see the kingdom of God."

Romans 8:29

For those whom he foreknew he also predestined to be conformed to the image of his Son, in order that he might be the firstborn among many brothers.

Colossians 3:9

Do not lie to one another, seeing that you have put off the old self with its practices.

LORD'S DAY 4

Q&A 9

Q. *But does not God do man an injustice by requiring in his law what man cannot do?*

A. No, for God so created man that he was able to do it. But man, at the instigation of the devil, in deliberate disobedience robbed himself and all his descendants of these gifts.

We must distinguish between innocent inability and culpable inability. When an employer assigns to his employee a particular task without supplying the necessary equipment, the employee is innocent if the job does not get done. But if an employee comes to work drunk, his inability is culpable. Such inability reflects unwillingness.

In Paradise, God had supplied everything necessary. But Adam listened to the devil. So no one can complain about God continuing to hold mankind accountable for his disobedience (Eccl. 12:13).

For Scripture teaches that we too were in Paradise. The entire human race constitutes an organic unity, not a collection of individuals. An individual is a distinct person, but no human being exists apart from one's ancestors and contemporaries. Scripture teaches that all human beings are of one blood (Acts 17:26).

Moreover, Adam was a special person. He was a real man, who received his wife from God, and together they received children. But Adam's relationship to every human being is compared by the apostle Paul with that of Christ to every believer.

Adam was God's vicegerent and God's vassal. In ancient times a vassal could be a great blessing for his people, but also a disaster, if, for example, he failed to honor the treaties he had entered into with his suzerain. This is how Adam's conduct brought God's wrath upon us, and because of it, every human being is born under this wrath, so that no one in their own strength can do what is good and avoid what is evil, unless through his Word and Spirit God provides a person with a new heart. This explains why every human being is subject to death. Indeed, one could mention more punishments, as we learn from Questions and Answers 10 and 11.

Q&A 10

Q. *Will God allow such disobedience and apostasy to go unpunished?*

A. Certainly not. He is terribly displeased with our original sin as well as our actual sins. Therefore he will punish them by a just judgment both now and eternally, as he has declared: "Cursed be everyone who does not abide by all things written in the Book of the Law" (Gal. 3:10).

Death is the enemy of every human being. Eventually death slays everyone (1 Cor. 15:26), not only the elderly but sometimes also children who are very young, some who are newborns, indeed, some even before they are born. Where does that come from? That comes from so-called original sin. Simply because we are children of Adam and Eve, we are all liable to death, children of death.

In addition, however, there are those sins that each person commits in their life for which they are accountable. These sins are sometimes called "actual sins," as in Answer 10 of the Heidelberg Catechism, for example: God "is terribly displeased with our original sin as well as our actual sins." Scripture informs us that we can sin in thought, words, and deeds.

So God's judgment upon every human being is fair, that is,

without discrimination or partiality. Indeed, God's wrath is provoked all the more toward people who know his commandment but have not obeyed it. Because they were priests, Nadab and Abihu were killed immediately (Lev. 10:1–2). It was said especially to God's covenant people that the Lord is a consuming fire and that it is terrifying to fall into the hands of the living God (Deut. 4:24; Ps. 76:8; Heb. 10:31; 12:29). No nation has experienced that as severely as Israel did when she was punished with exile (Lev. 26; Deut. 28–29; 2 Kgs. 17). In fact, if God's strict fairness is to be seen anywhere, then it must be seen in the suffering of his own beloved Son, our Lord Jesus Christ, as Mediator in our place. People who have known the gospel but not believed it will not see the life of eternal glory, for the wrath of God abides upon them (John 3:36). But in addition to punishing sin with eternal punishment in hell, God also visits temporal punishments upon sin here and now, such as sickness, war, famine, and finally death itself (Rom. 6:23).

Q&A 11

Q. *But is God not also merciful?*

A. God is indeed merciful, but he is also just. His justice requires that sin committed against the most high majesty of God also be punished with the most severe, that is, with everlasting, punishment of body and soul.

The word *justice* (= *righteousness*) appears in Scripture in a twofold sense, namely, as retributive justice and as redemptive justice.

Here and later, in Lord's Day 5, the Catechism uses the word in the former sense, in terms of retributive justice. (For redemptive justice, see Pss. 31:2; 71:2; 143:1; and Isa. 33:5.)

Here the Catechism is confessing that God does not treat the guilty as though they were innocent. That is why God punished Adam, though not immediately to the full extent. God is very patient. But when his forbearance reaches its end, he will cast all the wicked and unbelievers into hell. No one will escape that righteous punishment unless they believe in the Lord Jesus Christ as our Mediator. Jesus cried out on the cross, "My God, my God, why have you forsaken me?" (Matt. 27:46).

When we read here of the eternal punishment "of body and soul," many people see the phrase "body and soul" as referring to the entire person, inside and out. Practically speaking, that is unobjectionable. Consider the meaning of the expression as it appears, for example, in Matthew 10:28, where we read, "And do not fear those who kill the body but cannot kill the soul. Rather fear him who can destroy both soul and body in hell." We suggest, however, that in this verse the phrase "destroy both soul and body" means "destroy a person twice over."

In former times, the word *hell* was another word for "grave." In some English versions we read in Psalm 116:3 of "the pains of hell" (KJV), or "the terrors of Sheol" (NASB), or "the pangs of Sheol" (ESV), all of which mean "fear of the grave." Perhaps the poet who composed that psalm was feeling stricken. In Matthew 16:18 we also read of "the gates of hell," which refers to the power of death with which enemies threaten believers.

According to Matthew 10:28, our Lord Jesus once said that we must not fear enemies who in times of persecution can kill us, but that we should rather fear God who can destroy us in Gehenna. This word was originally the name of a particular valley near Jerusalem, one that was extremely unclean because unspeakable atrocities had once been committed there, such as the sacrifice of children. For that reason the ravine was used as a garbage dump. People dumped corpses there, and decomposing worms crawled around. Jesus derived his imagery from that ravine when he spoke about hell, "where their worm does not die and the fire is not quenched" (Mark 9:48). There, those who have been condemned will be afflicted with incessant agony and writhing because they chose evil rather than good (Rev. 20). Surely on that day God will make a distinction. Judas betrayed our Savior, but Pilate also left him in the lurch (John 19:11). In any case, on the day of judgment it will be more tolerable for pagans than for people like us, if we neglect or even despise and oppose God's covenant and commandments that were sealed by our baptism (Matt. 11:24; Luke 12:47–48). Such people are indeed liable to severe punishment.

Scripture References

Ecclesiastes 12:13

The end of the matter; all has been heard. Fear God and keep his commandments, for this is the whole duty of man.

Romans 5:12

Therefore, just as sin came into the world through one man, and death through sin, and so death spread to all men because all sinned.

Romans 5:14

Yet death reigned from Adam to Moses, even over those whose sinning was not like the transgression of Adam, who was a type of the one who was to come.

1 Cor. 15:21–22

For as by a man came death, by a man has come also the resurrection of the dead. For as in Adam all die, so also in Christ shall all be made alive.

LORD'S DAY 5

Q&A 12

Q. *Since, according to God's righteous judgment we deserve temporal and eternal punishment, how can we escape this punishment and be again received into favor?*

A. God demands that his justice be satisfied. Therefore we must make full payment, either by ourselves or through another.

Now begins the second part of the Catechism, dealing with our salvation.

When the Catechism uses the word *must* here and elsewhere (see Q&A 15), we may not conclude from this that some power above God gave God a command that, and how, he should punish sin. We must not go in that direction with our thinking.

In Scripture we read occasionally that there were unfaithful judges. They "perverted" justice, as did the sons of Samuel, for example. They took bribes and treated a poor person unfairly. Moses had warned about such things earlier: "Keep far from a false charge, and do not kill the innocent and righteous, for I will not acquit the wicked" (Exod. 23:7). And Proverbs 17:15 says, "He who justifies the wicked and he who condemns the righteous are both alike an abomination to the LORD."

Our God is fair. He does not treat the guilty as though they were innocent. As early as in Paradise, he immediately declared Adam guilty, and all his descendants together with him (Gen.

3:19; Rom. 5:12). The experience of every day has been demonstrating the truth of this for centuries.

Therefore the question arises: How can peace be obtained again between God and us? Can that really happen?

Yes, it can. We know that God has desired to reconcile the world to himself. He did so by satisfying his justice that had been violated, a satisfaction rendered by our Lord Jesus Christ.

Q&A 13

Q. *Can we by ourselves make this payment?*

A. Certainly not. On the contrary, we daily increase our debt.

When our Savior was on earth, a person occasionally would be burdened with such a large debt that he would be sentenced to prison. But that person could still be set free if someone else paid for him. That payment was called a "ransom."

One time Jesus himself used this kind of payment of a ransom when speaking of his payment for the debt of sin, a payment by which such a debt could be forgiven: "Even as the Son of Man came not to be served but to serve, and to give his life as a ransom for many" (Matt. 20:28).

The Catechism also compares the satisfaction of God's justice that had been violated so seriously by our sins with the payment of money for a debt. In reality, though, Scripture teaches that we have been saved by something altogether different from gold and silver. For we are saved by blood, the blood of Jesus Christ, God's Son (1 Pet. 1:18–19).

Throughout the centuries there have repeatedly been people who supposed that they themselves could contribute something to satisfying God's justice. In the days of Micah, for example, people asked whether they could please God with enormous sacrifices of calves, rams, and oil (Micah 6:6–7). During Jesus's sojourn on earth, the Pharisees presented themselves as being able, by their scrupulous keeping of various self-made commands, to amass a large supply of righteousness with God (Matt. 5:20; Phil.

3:9). The Jewish people who went over to the Christian church bringing this view with them continued to think they were justified at least partially through the works of the law (these were the Judaizers). They were opposed strenuously by the apostle Paul (Rom. 3:20; 8:3).

Who is so perfect as to be able to satisfy God's justice? The apostle James reminds his fellow Christians that we stumble daily in many things (Jas. 3:2).

Q&A 14

Q. *Can any mere creature pay for us?*

A. No. In the first place, God will not punish another creature for the sin that man has committed. Furthermore, no mere creature can sustain the burden of God's eternal wrath against sin and deliver others from it.

So we have seen that we cannot possibly save ourselves. Nor can we be saved by another creature that is nothing more than a creature. Our Lord Jesus was not, and is not, such a creature. He both was God and remained God at the same time when he became man. He arose from the grave by his own power (Rom. 1:4).

We had to be saved by a real creature, for the great rebellion against God had been committed by human beings. The payment had to come from human beings. During Old Testament times, the blood of animals was used, but it served to represent the work that God's Son would come to perform on earth (Heb. 2:14–15; 10:4). God himself thereby provided the means so that his church might possess divine instruction for creating and confirming faith in the gospel. This gospel was bestowed initially in shadows, but after being fulfilled by Christ, the apostles received the mandate to preach this gospel of fulfillment internationally (Matt. 28:18–20).

Even if there had been a perfect creature that had offered itself as the ransom for our guilt, it still could not have saved us. For such a creature would never have survived God's wrath. That creature would have suffered the second death. But our Lord

Jesus was able to bear and to endure that terrible wrath of God, because he was not only real man but also real God.

Q&A 15

Q. *What kind of mediator and deliverer must we seek?*

A. One who is a true and righteous man, and yet more powerful than all creatures; that is, one who is at the same time true God.

The way this question is formulated is not entirely felicitous. From the beginning of sin in Paradise, God himself provided salvation: "I will put enmity between you and the woman, and between your offspring and her offspring; he shall bruise your head, and you shall bruise his heel" (Gen. 3:15). So we need not look very far to find talk of a Mediator and Savior. We know him already, from the Bible. From Scripture we know that it pleased God to provide a Savior for us.

God's own Son offered himself voluntarily (Ps. 40:9; Rom. 8:32; Heb. 10:9–10). Our Savior is also called our Security. That is the term for someone who pays for another person.

Through his disobedience the first Adam brought under curse and death all those who with him constituted the body of humanity, but through his obedience the second Adam (that is, Christ) has obtained forgiveness of sins and eternal life for all who one day will constitute the one body of believers with him as the Head.

Scripture References

Romans 5:12
Therefore, just as sin came into the world through one man, and death through sin, and so death spread to all men because all sinned. . . .

1 Corinthians 15:20–22
But in fact Christ has been raised from the dead, the firstfruits of those who have fallen asleep. For as by a man came death, by a man has come also the resurrection of the dead. For as in Adam all die, so also in Christ shall all be made alive.

LORD'S DAY 6

The battle front against which Lord's Day 5 was fighting was that of Pharisaism, Judaizing, and Roman Catholicism. The confession of our need for a Savior continues in Lord's Day 6, this time to fight against the battle front of Anabaptism. Among the Anabaptists, some denied that God's Son had become a real human being in the same manner as we—that is, along the route of conception and birth. (For more about this, see Lord's Day 14.)

Q&A 16

Q. *Why must he be a true and righteous man?*

A. He must be a true man because the justice of God requires that the same human nature that has sinned should pay for sin. He must be a righteous man because one who himself is a sinner cannot pay for others.

Q&A 17

Q. *Why must he at the same time be true God?*

A. He must be true God so that by the power of his divine nature he might bear in his human nature the burden of God's wrath, and might obtain for us and restore to us righteousness and life.

(a) First, our Mediator had to be a real human being, for sin was introduced on earth by people, by the parents of us all, Adam and Eve. This explains why God can be satisfied with no payment other than with a human payment. Our Savior was born then as a real baby and was raised to be a real adult: "But when the fullness of time had come, God sent forth his Son, born of woman, born under the law, to redeem those who were under the law, so that we might receive adoption as sons" (Gal. 4:4–5); "For as [or: since] by a man came death, by a man has come also the resurrection of the dead" (1 Cor. 15:21).

(b) Next, our Mediator had to be a righteous human being: someone who perfectly kept God's commandments with his whole heart. In the law of shadows, for example, no sacrificial animal with any blemish was accepted, and no single sacrifice could be rendered without incense. A priest, for example, was not permitted to be disfigured (Lev. 21:17; 22:22): "For it was indeed fitting that we should have such a high priest, holy, innocent, unstained, separated from sinners, and exalted above the heavens. He has no need, like those high priests, to offer sacrifices daily, first for his own sins and then for those of the people, since he did this once for all when he offered up himself. For the law [of shadows] appoints men in their weakness as high priests, but the word of the oath, which came later than the law, appoints a Son who has been made perfect forever" (Heb. 7:26–28).

(c) Third, our Savior had to be real God. A Mediator who was merely a human being would have remained under God's eternal wrath. But a Mediator who was simultaneously real God could rise again from suffering and death through the power of his deity. Jesus said, "For this reason the Father loves me, because I lay down my life that I may take it up again. No one takes it from me, but I lay it down of my own accord. I have authority to lay it down, and I have authority to take it up again" (John 10:17–18). We are saved by the blood of him who is God's Son (Acts 20:28; 1 John 1:7).

Q&A 18

Q. *But who is that Mediator who at the same time is true God and a true and righteous man?*

A. Our Lord Jesus Christ, who has become for us wisdom from God—that is, our righteousness, holiness, and redemption (1 Cor. 1:30).

Later we will discuss more extensively the fact that Jesus satisfied three requirements: (a) he was real man, (b) he was sinless man, and (c) he was real God. At this point we will provide merely a brief summary.

(a) Jesus was truly man, that is, a real man. He was truly born according to the promise of Isaiah 9:6, he was part of the history of Bethlehem (Luke 2:6, etc.), and he grew up in Nazareth to become an adult man (Isa. 53:3; Acts 17:31). He ate and drank, walked and slept. He prayed often.

(b) The proclamation that he is God, specifically God's Son, constitutes the basis of the entire Gospel of John (1:1–3) and the like.

So then, God has granted us this Mediator for many purposes, of which the Catechism mentions the following four:

Given for our wisdom

The apostle Paul informs us that his listeners in Corinth initially found his preaching strange. It centered on a man who had been punished with the death of a criminal, crucifixion (1 Cor. 1:23). But the apostle showed that Jesus's horrible death has put to shame precisely the wisdom of the religion of the worldly wise men. For who ever came up with such an idea of saving sinners through the death of God's own Son? If those renowned scholars of the Sanhedrin in Jerusalem had understood only a small part of that, they would not crucified him who is now the Lord of glory (1 Cor. 1:20; 2:8).

Given for our righteousness

Our Savior is often called the Righteous One (Acts 3:14; 7:52; 22:14; 1 Pet. 4:18; 1 John 2:1). He perfectly obeyed God's will and therefore acquired an inexhaustible treasury of righteousness. The Holy Spirit grants us a share in this treasury by teaching us to believe in the gospel concerning Jesus Christ (see 1 Cor. 2:13). Scripture calls this our justification.

Given for our holiness

Our Savior is also frequently called the Holy One (Ps. 16:10; Isa. 41:14; Luke 1:35; 4:34; Acts 2:37; 4:27; 13:35). The apostle Peter calls him "the Holy and Righteous One" in one and the same breath (Acts 3:14). To sanctify means to separate from the world and dedicate to the service of God. For example, the altars and the sacrifices were sanctified, and so were the priests. Thus the Lord Jesus also sanctified himself when he surrendered himself for us in death both as a priest and as the sacrifice (John 17:19; Heb. 7:26). That was necessary for fulfilling the shadows of the law. But by submitting himself obediently to that severe requirement, Jesus obtained for us a perfect holiness "once for all" (Heb. 10:10). The Holy Spirit comes also to grant this holiness to Christians and their children in the promise of the gospel, to seal it through our baptism, and to cause us to appropriate it by moving our heart to faith in such a beloved holy Savior. When this holiness of Christ works itself out in the life of believers, Scripture calls this their sanctification (2 Thess. 2:13; see our comments on Lord's Day 3).

Given for a complete salvation

As long as we live, we experience the power of sin in various ways, in many shortcomings and trespasses, in sicknesses and in dying. But when our Savior returns, he will save us completely from all of this (Luke 21:28; Phil. 3:21; Rev. 7:16–17).

Q&A 19

Q. *From where do you know this?*

A. From the holy gospel, which God himself first revealed in Paradise. Later, he had it proclaimed by the patriarchs and prophets, and foreshadowed by the sacrifices and other ceremonies of the law. Finally, he had it fulfilled through his only Son.

(a) Everything that has been said about Christ up to this point we know not from people, but from God. It was the Holy Spirit himself who had this proclaimed and written down by prophets and apostles (1 Thess. 2:13; 2 Tim. 3:16; 2 Pet. 1:19–21; Rev. 22:18–19). From this we know that God himself made the gospel known in Paradise. In Genesis 3:15 he said to the serpent (which was being used by Satan): I will put enmity between you and this woman, between your seed (your party, your followers, Matt. 3:7) and her seed (that is, the human race, especially Christ, Heb. 2:11, 14; Rev. 12:5); this One (that is, Christ) will bruise your head (on Golgotha Satan was defeated, Col. 2:15) and you shall bruise his heel (crush the body, render it powerless, which happened at Christ's death and burial). These words of God are called the *mother promise*, because all subsequent promises flow from this one.

(b) From the same Holy Scripture we know that God provided for the coming of Christ to be "proclaimed" by prophets like Moses, David, Isaiah, and Micah. These men could not do that of themselves, but it was the Spirit of Christ who bore witness ahead of time about the suffering that Christ would bear and the glory that would follow thereafter (1 Pet. 1:11–12). People should read David's Psalm 22 (Christ humiliated by God, but also exalted by him), Isaiah 53 (about the suffering and conquering Servant of the Lord), and Micah 5:1 (that the Messiah would be born in Bethlehem). On the day of his resurrection the Lord Jesus himself showed the travelers to Emmaus that the Old Testament (which is our phrase for the first three-quarters of the Bible) was filled with teaching about the Messiah, about Christ, that he would suffer, die, and be victorious (Luke 24:13–35; John 21:22).

(c) God arranged for the work that Christ would come to perform to be "foreshadowed by the sacrifices and other ceremonies of the law." The law supplied visual instruction by means of altars, priests, sacrifices, and blood, whereby God wanted to teach Israel how sinful and guilty she was, so that she could be saved from temporal punishment and eternal condemnation only through God's mercy. Ceremonies mean shadows. For example, every lamb, as it was slaughtered at the tabernacle or temple, was a picture of Christ (John 1:29). Every priest was a shadow of Christ, our High Priest (Heb. 8:1). Aaron's entering into the holy of holies on the great Day of Atonement was a shadow of Christ's ascension when he would appear before God for us (Heb. 9:24). We are now privileged to understand the scope of the Old Testament shadows more clearly than the Israelite church of old did. In addition to the shadow we see also the substance (namely, Christ, Col. 2:17). God used those ancient shadows as a "guardian until Christ came" (Gal. 3:24). The apostle uses the word *paidagōgos*, from which our word *pedagogy* (the study of teaching) is derived. The law with its shadows was like a picture book from which the immature (Jewish) church received instruction in God's grace through Christ. See also the beautiful epistle to the Hebrews (now we have no image but reality, Heb. 10:1). And recall John 1:17: "For the law was given through Moses; grace and truth came through Jesus Christ." The Catechism is quite correct in saying that God saw to it that the gospel was "foreshadowed by the sacrifices and other ceremonies of the law. Finally, he had it fulfilled through his only Son" (see Heb. 1:1).

Scripture References

Genesis 3:15
> "I will put enmity between you and the woman,
>   and between your offspring and her offspring;
> he shall bruise your head,
>   and you shall bruise his heel."

Luke 24:13-47

That very day two of them were going to a village named Emmaus, about seven miles from Jerusalem, and they were talking with each other about all these things that had happened. While they were talking and discussing together, Jesus himself drew near and went with them. But their eyes were kept from recognizing him. And he said to them, "What is this conversation that you are holding with each other as you walk?" And they stood still, looking sad. Then one of them, named Cleopas, answered him, "Are you the only visitor to Jerusalem who does not know the things that have happened there in these days?" And he said to them, "What things?" And they said to him, "Concerning Jesus of Nazareth, a man who was a prophet mighty in deed and word before God and all the people, and how our chief priests and rulers delivered him up to be condemned to death, and crucified him. But we had hoped that he was the one to redeem Israel. Yes, and besides all this, it is now the third day since these things happened. Moreover, some women of our company amazed us. They were at the tomb early in the morning, and when they did not find his body, they came back saying that they had even seen a vision of angels, who said that he was alive. Some of those who were with us went to the tomb and found it just as the women had said, but him they did not see." And he said to them, "O foolish ones, and slow of heart to believe all that the prophets have spoken! Was it not necessary that the Christ should suffer these things and enter into his glory?" And beginning with Moses and all the Prophets, he interpreted to them in all the Scriptures the things concerning himself.

So they drew near to the village to which they were going. He acted as if he were going farther, but they urged him strongly, saying, "Stay with us, for it is toward evening and the day is now far spent." So he went in to stay with them. When he was at table with them, he took the bread and blessed and broke it and gave it to them. And their eyes were opened, and they recognized him. And he vanished from their sight. They said to each other, "Did not our hearts burn within us while he talked to us on the road, while he opened to us the Scriptures?" And they rose that same hour and returned to Jerusalem. And they found the eleven and those who were with them gathered together, saying, "The Lord has risen indeed, and has appeared to Simon!" Then they told what had happened on the road, and how he was known to them in the breaking of the bread.

As they were talking about these things, Jesus himself stood among them, and said to them, "Peace to you!" But they were startled and frightened and thought they saw a spirit. And he said to them, "Why are you troubled, and why do doubts arise in your hearts? See my hands and my feet, that it is I myself. Touch me, and see. For a spirit does not have flesh and bones as you see that I have." And when he had said this, he showed them his hands and his feet. And while they still disbelieved for joy and were marveling, he said to them, "Have you anything here to eat?" They gave him a piece of broiled fish, and he took it and ate before them.

Then he said to them, "These are my words that I spoke to you while I was still with you, that everything written about me in the Law of Moses and the Prophets and the Psalms must be fulfilled." Then he opened their minds to understand the Scriptures, and said to them, "Thus it is written, that the Christ should suffer and on the third day rise from the dead, and that repentance and forgiveness of sins should be proclaimed in his name to all nations, beginning from Jerusalem."

Romans 8:3-4
For God has done what the law, weakened by the flesh, could not do. By sending his own Son in the likeness of sinful flesh and for sin, he condemned sin in the flesh, in order that the righteous requirement of the law might be fulfilled in us, who walk not according to the flesh but according to the Spirit.

1 Corinthians 1:20
Where is the one who is wise? Where is the scribe? Where is the debater of this age? Has not God made foolish the wisdom of the world?

Colossians 2:17
These are a shadow of the things to come, but the substance belongs to Christ.

Hebrews 7:26
For it was indeed fitting that we should have such a high priest, holy, innocent, unstained, separated from sinners, and exalted above the heavens.

1 John 1:7
But if we walk in the light, as he is in the light, we have fellowship with one another, and the blood of Jesus his Son cleanses us from all sin.

LORD'S DAY 7

Q&A 20

Q. *Are all men, then, saved by Christ just as they perished through Adam?*

A. No. Only those are saved who by a true faith are grafted into Christ and accept all his benefits.

Through the sin of Adam the entire world became liable to punishment before God (Rom. 3:19, 23). But in this we see how great God's love is, since he gave his own Son as a Mediator so that everyone who believes in him might not perish but have eternal life (John 3:16; 1 John 4:9).

To bring people to this faith, God causes his gospel to be preached to such nations and at such times as he himself determines in his sovereignty. There was a time when he wanted to maintain his covenant exclusively with Israel, but that time is past, and now people from pagan backgrounds may share in God's covenant—we and our children (Rom. 4:17; 15:9; Gal. 3:7, 14; Eph. 3:3–6; 1 Pet. 2:10).

But not all who are called by the gospel accept it with heartfelt faith. That happened already when Jesus himself was still on earth, so that Jesus complained, "How often would I have gathered your [Jerusalem's] children together as a hen gathers her brood under her wings, and you were not willing!" (Matt. 23:37).

But all who do believe in Christ constitute one body, similar to being engrafted together. The Lord Jesus is the Head of that body and the believers are its members (Eph. 1:22–23). He is the Bridegroom and the believers are his bride (John 3:29; Rev. 21:9). If a husband is wealthy, so is his wife. Similarly, the members of Christ's body share in the glory that their Head possesses now already. Indeed, here on earth they already receive righteousness and holiness from him, but when he returns they will receive complete salvation (see our discussion of Q&A 18, concerning righteousness and holiness).

Q&A 21

Q. *What is true faith?*

A. True faith is a sure knowledge whereby I accept as true all that God has revealed to us in his Word. At the same time it is a firm confidence that not only to others, but also to me, God has granted forgiveness of sins, everlasting righteousness, and salvation, out of mere grace, only for the sake of Christ's merits. This faith the Holy Spirit works in my heart by the gospel.

Here the Catechism discusses true faith. For there are also such things as untrue faith, false faith, and imitation faith. People also speak of living faith in contrast to dead faith.

Faith is the most characteristically human feature that exists. Animals cannot believe. But all people place a certain religious trust in something or someone, to which they ascribe great power and from which they expect good or fear evil. In Isaiah 44 Scripture tells us about pagans who first make a god for themselves from a piece of a tree and use the rest of the tree for cooking their meal. Our own ancestors did something like that as well. Nowadays many people pay homage to an idol in the form of money and possessions, prestige and science, etc., and expect all of their well-being from such idols. But we can have no respect for such misplaced trust. When Paul saw that Athens was filled with the images of idols, he did not praise those pagans for that; rather, "his spirit was provoked within him" and he told them the truth about God and about our Savior Jesus Christ (Acts

17). The prophet from Judah would not permit himself in any way to participate in the idolatrous activities of King Jeroboam, though the latter praised the golden calf as the god who had delivered Israel from Egypt (1 Kings 13). Then in the time of Isaiah, the church people were very busy sacrificing and praying in the temple but were also violating justice by oppressing widows and orphans, etc. The Lord said that he had had enough of such piety (Isa. 1:11). Paul called the faith of false teachers in Colossae fleshly (Col. 2:11, 23). James called the faith of church members who dealt without love toward the poor, widows, etc., an empty religion and dead faith (Jas. 1:26–27; 2:17, 26). He mentioned that the demons also possess such dead faith, "and shudder!" Scripture frequently tells us about people who were inclined to see Jesus as having attractive qualities but who did not remain faithful to him (John 2:23–24; 12:42–43).

But we also read frequently in Scripture about the true faith that pleases God. Whereas everyone opposed Jesus, including his own disciples at times (for he refused to be an earthly messiah wearing a crown), Jesus placed his exclusive trust in the Word of God. From this he knew that the Messiah had to suffer before entering into glory (Luke 24:26). Even when he hung on the cross, Jesus continued holding firmly to God's promise, even though he was scorned because of that trust in God (Ps. 22:8; Matt. 27:43). This is why he is called "the founder and perfecter of our faith" in Hebrews 12:2.

Scripture shows us other examples of true faith, though less glorious, in the stories of Abel, Noah, Abraham, and others, for whom faith was "the assurance of things hoped for, the conviction of things not seen" (Heb. 11:1). In particular, Abraham is mentioned extensively. In the Hebrew of Genesis 15:6, we are literally told that he said "amen" to God's promise.

So true faith is entirely different from the faith people sometimes talk about when they think it is raining: "I believe that it is raining." That is doubtful talk. Rather, the faith that the Catechism is discussing is the direct opposite of doubt (Rom. 4:20; Jas. 1:6). According to Scripture, to believe is to accept unconditionally everything that God says in Holy Scripture, in terms of its discussion, for example, that God created the universe (Heb.

11:3), or the history of the nations (Deut. 32:8), or regarding the future of the church and the judgment on the last day.

But in the New Testament, to believe often means substantially to believe in Christ. For that matter, in terms of its character, this faith is the same faith as that of Abraham. Everything God foretold in the Old Testament is fulfilled in Christ (2 Cor. 1:20).

Practically speaking, when Scripture speaks of true faith, it often means believing in the Lord Jesus. It often describes true faith as obedience to Christ or to the gospel (John 3:36; Rom. 1:5; 10:16; 2 Thess. 1:8).

Another word for "faith" is *acceptance* (that is, of Christ or his gospel, John 1:11–12; Acts 2:41; 1 Cor. 15:1; Col. 2:6; 1 Tim. 1:15). Indeed, to believe is at one point described as eating the flesh of the Lord Jesus and drinking his blood (see John 6:54)—which means to accept with a believing heart the entire suffering and death of Christ, and thereby to receive forgiveness of sins and eternal life. Our young children can say that God has sealed this promise to them as well through their baptism.

Not everyone always perseveres in this true faith with equal faithfulness. In Holy Scripture some people receive a good testimony, like Abel (Heb. 11:4), Abraham (Rom. 4:20), the Gentile centurion of Capernaum (Matt. 8:10), and the Canaanite woman to whom Jesus said, "O woman, great is your faith!" (Matt. 15:28). But others, including some among the disciples, Jesus scolded when he called them people of little faith (Matt. 6:30; 8:26; 14:31; 17:20; Luke 24:25). Within one and the same believer, true faith at times perseveres and at other times wanes. As a rule Abraham trusted in God's promise (which was his righteousness, Gen. 15:6), but at Sarah's insistence he took Hagar as a concubine (Gen. 16). The disciples asked straight out for an increase of their faith (Luke 17:5), and the Lord Jesus prayed for Peter that his faith would not fail (Luke 22:32).

Concerning this true faith, Scripture teaches that God works it in us (Phil. 2:13). We read as well that the Holy Spirit uses means, such as other people. For example, the Corinthians were brought to faith in Christ through the labor of Paul and Apollos (1 Cor. 3:5). We must pay attention to both the Word and the Spirit.

The apostle writes that faith is worked in us through God's Word, for example, in Romans 10:14, 17. Faith comes from hearing, and hearing comes through the Word of God. The apostle also calls the gospel the power of God for salvation (Rom. 1:16; see also Isa. 55:11; 2 Cor. 2:15–16; Eph. 6:17).

But Scripture also teaches that the Word of God is preached by no one less than the Holy Spirit. That happened already in Old Testament times. It was the Holy Spirit who equipped Moses, David, and other prophets to speak the word of God (1 Pet. 1:11–12; 2 Pet. 1:21). But this is even more evident in the New Testament. Paul writes that no one can say Jesus is Lord except through the Holy Spirit (1 Cor. 12:3). He calls God's Word simply "the sword of the Spirit" (Eph. 6:17).

In addition, the church is here confessing that the Holy Spirit makes us believe that not only to others, but also to each of us personally forgiveness of sins, eternal righteousness, and holiness are granted. With this, the Catechism means that faith possesses a personal element. Each believer must believe for himself or herself. We cannot believe for someone else. For example, none of us should not say that we believe everything that the church believes despite knowing little or nothing of what the church believes. We ourselves must accept Christ and his benefits (John 4:42). Even though we confess that faith is a gift of God (Phil. 2:13), it is nevertheless also something that must be done by us. Specifically, it is a work of our heart (Rom. 10:10). Our heart is the center of our person, from which come all our thoughts, desires, words, deeds, and the like. If the heart of a person is not obedient toward God, then everything we think and do is evil at its deepest level (Mark 7:20–23). When as a Pharisee Paul trusted in his scrupulous view of the law and performance of the law, he was just as dead in sins and trespasses as the Ephesians who at that point were trusting in their idol gods. Only when God's Spirit moves us to true faith in Christ does our heart become different and all our activities become different as well. This is the justification (forgiveness of sins) and sanctification (regeneration) that we spoke about earlier.

We discussed justification earlier in connection with Question and Answer 18 and will discuss it again later in connection with Lord's Day 23.

We discussed salvation earlier in connection with Lord's Day 6, Question and Answer 18: "sanctification and complete salvation." When the Ephesians were still pagans and idol worshipers, they were "dead in the trespasses and sins" (Eph. 2:1). It is also the same with us "by nature" (v. 3). If baptized children are not instructed in the gospel, they will sooner commit evil than do good. But if the Holy Spirit moves us, through our parents or other Christians, to faith in our beloved Savior, then through that faith our heart is cleansed and renewed (Acts 15:7–9). This is what the apostle was referring to when he wrote, "For by grace you have been saved through faith" (Eph. 2:8), and he called this "the life of God" (Eph. 4:18). One day that salvation will be complete, when we are raised from the dead by Jesus (Rom. 8:11).

Q&A 22

Q. *What, then, must a Christian believe?*

A. All that is promised us in the gospel, which the articles of our catholic and undoubted Christian faith teach us in a summary.

If the Lord Jesus were still on earth, we could go to him and fall down at his feet and listen to his voice. But he is now in heaven, and we owe everything that we know about him to the Holy Spirit who has seen to it that everything we must know about Jesus was revealed. Without Christ there would be no Bible. The Bible does not simply speak here and there in a few disconnected Messianic verses that appear incidentally, scattered about like some errant stones, but without Christ the Bible would not exist. Anyone wanting to write a book about the coming of Christ will have to start with the mother promise in Paradise. He would also have to indicate how the land of Canaan had already been given in the promise made to Abraham and to the Israelites, the promise that was later fulfilled. In the same way Christ and his benefits are bestowed in the promise, a promise sealed already to an infant.

Therefore the Catechism says correctly that we must believe "all that is promised us in the gospel." Just as with the term *believe*, so with the term *promise*: it is not meant in its everyday use (as many equate making a promise with being uncertain). In the popular mind, promising can be a form of deception, since many people promise much and deliver little. No, here in Answer 22 the word *promise* is meant just as seriously as Scripture also means it, when it accuses someone who despises God's promise through unbelief of being a person who "has trampled underfoot the Son of God, and has profaned the blood of the covenant by which he was sanctified, and has outraged the Spirit of grace" (Heb. 10:29). For that reason one can say that God has given us the whole Christ wrapped in the promises of the gospel, just as you present a person with a gift that is wrapped in a box. True faith opens the box and takes Christ our Savior for oneself.

The church has formulated a summary of all that God promises us in his Word, a summary that consists of the twelve articles of our catholic and undoubted Christian faith. An article is like a member or a part, and the entire Christian doctrine is, as it were, one body that consists of twelve body parts.

Q&A 23

Q. What are these articles?

A.
I. 1. I believe in God the Father almighty, Creator of heaven and earth.

II. 2. I believe in Jesus Christ, his only-begotten Son, our Lord;

3. he was conceived by the Holy Spirit, born of the virgin Mary;

4. suffered under Pontius Pilate, was crucified, dead, and buried; he descended into hell.

5. On the third day he arose from the dead;

6. he ascended into heaven, and sits at the right hand of God the Father almighty;

(continued on next page)

Q&A 23 *(continued)*

7. from there he will come to judge the living and the dead.
 III. 8. I believe in the Holy Spirit;
      9. I believe a holy catholic Christian church, the communion of saints;
  10. the forgiveness of sins;
  11. the resurrection of the body;
  12. and the life everlasting.

These twelve articles are also called the Apostles' Creed. This confession did not receive the adjective "apostles'" because it was composed by the twelve apostles. It arose gradually, and initially was expressed in one locale somewhat differently than in another locale. It contained confessional formulations that arose from answers to questions asked of pagans, those who came to be baptized in the name of the Father, the Son, and the Holy Spirit (see Matt. 28:19–20).

In what follows we will return periodically to this confession and its history.

Scripture References

Genesis 15:6
And he believed the LORD, and he counted it to him as righteousness.

Habakkuk 2:4
    Behold, his soul is puffed up; it is not upright within him,
       but the righteous shall live by his faith.

John 3:16
"For God so loved the world, that he gave his only Son, that whoever believes in him should not perish but have eternal life."

John 3:36
Whoever believes in the Son has eternal life; whoever does not obey the Son shall not see life, but the wrath of God remains on him.

Romans 10:14
How then will they call on him in whom they have not believed? And how are they to believe in him of whom they have never heard? And how are they to hear without someone preaching?

Romans 10:17
So faith comes from hearing, and hearing through the word of Christ.

James 1:18
Of his own will he brought us forth by the word of truth, that we should be a kind of firstfruits of his creatures.

LORD'S DAY 8

Q&A 24

Q. *How are these articles divided?*

A. Into three parts: the first is about God the Father and our creation; the second about God the Son and our redemption; the third about God the Holy Spirit and our sanctification.

In connection with Lord's Day 7 we observed that the church has briefly summarized her doctrine about God the Father, God the Son, and God the Holy Spirit in twelve parts. That made it easy to remember.

When they came over to Christianity, pagans also had to testify to their agreement with the twelve articles if they wanted to be baptized. So the sequence was directly the opposite of what we follow. We are born as children of Christians, and therefore we are beneficiaries of the Word that applied to our parents, grandparents, and great-grandparents: "the promise is for you and for your children" (Acts 2:39), and baptism is the seal of that promise.

In the first section of her apostolic confession, the church speaks about the Father. Concerning the Father of our Lord Jesus Christ we confess that he created heaven and earth. We'll say more about this with Lord's Day 10.

In the second part of the confession, the church confesses that Jesus Christ is the Son of the Father. He is also called the Word (in Greek, *logos*). The church also confesses that the Son of God became man, and in this way he became our Savior through his suffering, death, and resurrection.

In the third section of the twelve articles, we confess the Holy Spirit. He is the one who moves us by the preaching of God's Word to believe in the Triune God, whereby our heart is sanctified and we turn away from the world in every respect and begin to live for God's honor.

Notice how intimately we are bound to these three—Father, Son, and Holy Spirit. We already are bound publicly by our baptism. At the end of several apostolic epistles, Scripture reminds us of this, when, for example, in 2 Corinthians 13:13–14 we are blessed in the name of the Father, the Son, and the Holy Spirit. Let us simply bring to mind each day that baptism which was administered on our foreheads.

Q&A 25

Q. *Since there is only one God, why do you speak of three persons, Father, Son, and Holy Spirit?*

A. Because God has so revealed himself in his Word that these three distinct persons are the one, true, eternal God.

Scripture teaches us that God alone is God, and no one else or nothing else is God. An idol is no god, and in Scripture we often read that God mocked such idols when he dealt with his people. He caused Dagon to fall on his nose before the ark (1 Sam. 5), and Elijah asked whether Baal was perhaps taking his afternoon nap (1 Kgs. 18). But the Lord is truly God.

With respect to God, Scripture informs us that he is *eternal*, that he is and remains God:

> Lord, you have been our dwelling place
> in all generations.
> Before the mountains were brought forth,
> or ever you had formed the earth and the world,
> from everlasting to everlasting you are God (Ps. 90:1–2)

In the Lord's Prayer (taught to us by Jesus himself) we say to God: "For yours is the kingdom and the power and the glory forever."

Regarding this God, we also know that he is *almighty*. Jesus said that the things that are impossible for man are possible with God (see Luke 18:27). God created heaven and earth and also upholds and rules all things.

God is also *omniscient*. He plumbs even our heart (Ps. 139). No creature is hidden before him, for all things lie open and uncovered before the eyes of him to whom we will give account (see Heb. 4:13).

Scripture also teaches us about God's *faithfulness*, also called God's *truth*. Read, for example, the story of Moses and the burning bush (Exod. 3). The Israelites were being oppressed in Egypt. But they had also participated in Egyptian idolatry (Josh. 24:14; Ezek. 16:26; 20:7–8; 23:19). But when they turned to God, the LORD acknowledged them as the posterity of Abraham, Isaac, and Jacob, and he remembered his promise to those patriarchs, that he would help their children out of their predicament (Gen. 15:13; Exod. 2:24–25). Therefore God said then that he would perform all that he had promised: "Say this to the people of Israel, 'I AM has sent me to you'" (Exod. 3:14).

In Hebrew the phrase "I AM" is pronounced approximately like *Yahweh*. During the Middle Ages this was turned into *Jehovah*. The meaning of that name is that God is the unchangingly faithful God of the covenant that he made with Abraham, Isaac, and Jacob, and their children. We too live under that covenant. The LORD has already fulfilled much of it—for example, the deliverance from Egypt, the inheriting of the land of Canaan—and Abraham has become the father of many believers from among the Gentiles (Rom. 4:11; Gal. 3:8).

So all Scripture is a book about God.

But at the same time Scripture teaches us (1) that God *alone* is God, and (2) that we must confess not only the Father as God, but also the Son and the Holy Spirit as God. We will discuss this more extensively later. At this point, let us hold firmly to the truth that these three Persons—Father, Son, and Holy Spirit—are three all equally God, each of the three no less than the other two.

This last claim, however, was contradicted by a certain man named Arius, who lived about 300 years after Christ and had a large following. He taught that the Father alone was completely God, but the Son and the Holy Spirit were made by the Father. They were made before creation, to be sure. He also claimed that the Father had created the world through the Son and the Holy Spirit. So they were not creatures as we are, but they were half-gods, intermediate beings between God and the world, and through these beings God then made that world.

The Christian church condemned that Arian doctrine and confessed straightforwardly that the Father, the Son, and the Holy Spirit are completely equal as God, that each of them is entirely God, as much as the others are.

At approximately the same time, there was a man named Sabellius, who held so firmly to the unity between Father, Son, and Holy Spirit that he refused to acknowledge any distinction between them. According to Sabellius, the one God functioned in the creation as Father, in salvation as the Son, and finally he lived in our hearts as the Holy Spirit. Some Sabellians even argued that the Father had hung on the cross.

In opposition to this foolishness, Scripture teaches clearly that the Father is entirely not the same as the Son, that the Son was sent and the Son became incarnate. Just as the Son is not the same as the Father, the Lord Jesus is not the same as the Holy Spirit. When he was about to depart from the earth, Jesus said that the Father would send another Comforter (John 14:16, 26). Therefore the church at that time maintained, against the Sabellians, that the Father, the Son, and the Holy Spirit are three, and called them three Persons.

So the church rejected the claims of both Arius and Sabellius. It did that by using the word *tri-unity*, or *trinity*. The "tri" was against the Sabellians, the "unity" was against the Arians. Even though the word *trinity* is not in the Bible, we must appreciate the good intention behind it. We should not stumble over a word, but focus on the issue. Eventually we will come to see that Scripture is full of the content which that word seeks to teach. Read, for example, Matthew 12. And another time, when our Savior was teaching in the temple, he pointed out that the scribes always had spoken about the Messiah alone as the Son of David; but in Psalm 110, the Savior said, David confessed the Messiah as his God, with the words "The Lord [Yahweh] said to my Lord . . ." (Mark 12:35–37). The Lord Jesus indicated by this that he was not only Son of David, but also Son of God.

There are more passages like this. For example, we must read Psalm 2 (regarding the king of Zion, the church) in the light of Acts 13:33; Hebrews 1:5; 5:5; and Isaiah 61, the latter of which was read in the synagogue of Nazareth by Jesus himself as being fulfilled in him. In the Gospels we read that the Son was sent into the world by the Father, that as a baby he was conceived by the virgin Mary from the Holy Spirit, that the Father honored him publicly as his Son, that the Holy Spirit descended upon him, and that before his departure to heaven God's Son commanded his apostles that believers and their children are to be baptized in the name of all three persons of the Godhead.

Scripture References

Psalm 86:10
For you are great and do wondrous things; you alone are God.

Ecclesiastes 5:1
Guard your steps when you go to the house of God. To draw near to listen is better than to offer the sacrifice of fools, for they do not know that they are doing evil.

Isaiah 63:7–19
"I will recount the steadfast love of the LORD,
    the praises of the LORD,
according to all that the LORD has granted us,
    and the great goodness to the house of Israel
that he has granted them according to his compassion,
    according to the abundance of his steadfast love.
For he said, "Surely they are my people,
    children who will not deal falsely."
    And he became their Savior.
In all their affliction he was afflicted,
    and the angel of his presence saved them;

in his love and in his pity he redeemed them;
    he lifted them up and carried them all the days of old.

But they rebelled
    and grieved his Holy Spirit;
therefore he turned to be their enemy,
    and himself fought against them.
Then he remembered the days of old,
    of Moses and his people.
Where is he who brought them up out of the sea
    with the shepherds of his flock?
Where is he who put in the midst of them
    his Holy Spirit,
who caused his glorious arm
    to go at the right hand of Moses,
who divided the waters before them
    to make for himself an everlasting name,
    who led them through the depths?
Like a horse in the desert,
    they did not stumble.
Like livestock that go down into the valley,
    the Spirit of the LORD gave them rest.
So you led your people,
    to make for yourself a glorious name.

Look down from heaven and see,
    from your holy and beautiful habitation.
Where are your zeal and your might?
    The stirring of your inner parts and your compassion
    are held back from me.
For you are our Father,
    though Abraham does not know us,
    and Israel does not acknowledge us;
you, O LORD, are our Father,
    our Redeemer from of old is your name.
O LORD, why do you make us wander from your ways
    and harden our heart, so that we fear you not?
Return for the sake of your servants,
    the tribes of your heritage.
Your holy people held possession for a little while;
    our adversaries have trampled down your sanctuary.

> We have become like those over whom you have never ruled,
>   like those who are not called by your name."

John 1:18

No one has ever seen God; the only God, who is at the Father's side, he has made him known.

Revelation 1:4–5

"John to the seven churches that are in Asia: Grace to you and peace from him who is and who was and who is to come, and from the seven spirits who are before his throne, and from Jesus Christ the faithful witness, the firstborn of the dead, and the ruler of kings on earth. To him who loves us and has freed us from our sins by his blood."

LORD'S DAY 9

Q&A 26

Q. *What do you believe when you say: I believe in God the Father almighty, Creator of heaven and earth?*

A. That the eternal Father of our Lord Jesus Christ, who out of nothing created heaven and earth and all that is in them and who still upholds and governs them by his eternal counsel and providence, is, for the sake of Christ his Son, my God and my Father. In him I trust so completely as to have no doubt that he will provide me with all things necessary for body and soul, and will also turn to my good whatever adversity he sends me in this life of sorrow. He is able to do so as almighty God, and willing also as a faithful Father.

When the apostle John planned to begin writing his Gospel and to narrate how he had genuinely walked and talked with Jesus, he began with an introduction (John 1:1–18) in which he stated that this same Lord Jesus was God, that he was the Logos. This Greek term *logos*, whose meaning in our language is rendered by the term *Word*, is masculine in Greek but neuter in English. By using the term *Logos* John was not suggesting in his introduction that he was going to write about an "it," but about a "he." Every reader of John's Gospel should remember that.

In your mind you should translate that term *Logos* as if it means *Speaker*, but in any case remember that it refers to a Person. And as you read, you should realize that John was claiming that this Speaker was God, and that all things were created through him. Furthermore, remember that John and the other disciples lived as close to him as Moses had lived with the tabernacle, and that they experienced that he was full of grace and truth (that is, full of love, benevolence, and faithfulness). This is how Jesus lived (literally from the Greek, *tabernacled*) among the disciples, and they beheld his glory and observed that he was a true Son of his Father, who also was full of grace and truth. Therefore it was no blasphemy for Jesus to say, "I and the Father are one," and it was not arrogant of him when he endeavored that people should believe that the Father was in him and he in the Father (John 10:38).

At times we say of someone, "He looks just like his father" (speaking, for example, of a minister).

The man Jesus Christ was the same as the Son of God, who was God himself. Therefore the Catechism correctly speaks of "the eternal Father of our Lord Jesus Christ," for when we honor the Son as the eternal God, we also thereby honor the Father (John 5:23; 1 John 2:23). For an eternal Son has an eternal Father.

God did not need the creation for this fatherhood. He made use of creation in order to save the crown of his creation—namely, the race of Adam and Eve, the human race—from perdition and condemnation. The Father sent his Son (John 3:16) and according to his wise counsel surrendered him to death for our salvation (Acts 2:23; Rom. 8:32). This explains why the Catechism goes on to confess that this eternal Father "is, for the sake of Christ his Son, my God and my Father."

As soon as we open the Bible, God's Spirit (who has given the Bible to us) shows us how powerful our heavenly Father is. The Father created heaven and earth. In the course of history, however, people have repeatedly thought in different ways about this. But let's not dispute long about this, for no human being was present at creation. Nor need we dispute about the reasons why God created everything. It pleased him to do that (Rev. 4:11). This must be enough for us. We can indeed learn from "the book of nature" how powerful our heavenly Father is. Consider the smallest animal—and try to make one yourself! He set in place the largest islands—Java, Borneo—like dust (Isa. 40:15). God said to Job, "Where were you when I laid the foundation of the earth?" (Job 38:4). Paul wrote, "Will what is molded say to its molder, 'Why have you made me like this?'" (Rom. 9:20).

It is therefore unbecoming for us to grant the title of "father" to popes, influential authors (like the "church fathers"), or the "fathers" of Dort (see Matt. 23:9). Nor should we be all that afraid of another person (Isa. 51:12–13). But when Abraham feared that he would die without leaving children behind, God showed him the innumerable stars and said, "So shall your offspring be." When Abraham trusted entirely in the LORD, that pleased God very much (Gen. 15:5; see Ps. 146:5–6). God can send us adversity for our advantage, as he did with Joseph (Gen. 45:8; 50:20). Our ancestors often died young, and called life "a continual dying" (see the Form for Baptism) and their existence "a vale of tears." But we can know that for those who love God all things work together for good (Rom. 8:28).

In connection with Lord's Day 10 we will see that evil people are culpable for their wicked deeds, but that nonetheless everything happens according to God's counsel, that is, his plan and good pleasure (Isa. 46:10). God rules according to a plan, not by accident. Everything happens according to his unfathomable wisdom and power, but each person is personally responsible for his or her actions. God's counsel does not make us "blocks and stones" (see Canons of Dort III/IV, art. 16). God is great and we do not comprehend him (Job 36:26).

In order to achieve his plan for his church, God has given everyone and everything a place, appointed and ordained beforehand. Nothing happens outside his will, although we human beings remain accountable and responsible.

Scripture References

Isaiah 40:26
> Lift up your eyes on high and see:
>   who created these?
> He who brings out their host by number,
>   calling them all by name,
> by the greatness of his might,
>   and because he is strong in power
>   not one is missing.

John 1:1–3

In the beginning was the Word, and the Word was with God, and the Word was God. He was in the beginning with God. All things were made through him, and without him was not any thing made that was made.

Romans 8:28

And we know that for those who love God all things work together for good, for those who are called according to his purpose.

Romans 8:30

And those whom he predestined he also called, and those whom he called he also justified, and those whom he justified he also glorified.

Ephesians 1:5

He predestined us for adoption as sons through Jesus Christ, according to the purpose of his will.

Revelation 4:11

> "Worthy are you, our Lord and God,
>> to receive glory and honor and power,
> for you created all things,
>> and by your will they existed and were created."

Lord's Day 10

Q&A 27

Q. *What do you understand by the providence of God?*

A. God's providence is his almighty and ever present power, whereby, as with his hand, he still upholds heaven and earth and all creatures, and so governs them that leaf and blade, rain and drought, fruitful and barren years, food and drink, health and sickness, riches and poverty, indeed, all things, come to us not by chance but by his fatherly hand.

In history we come across the term *Deism*. One can see immediately that it is derived from the Latin noun *Deus*, which means *God*. Thinkers and writers who were called Deists advocated the idea that God created heaven and earth but thereafter looked after it only occasionally, almost like someone who has made an old-fashioned watch or clock, wound it, and then looks at it only now and then. God ceased creating after six days (Gen. 1–2). But Jesus said, "My Father is working until now" (John 5:17).

So we need to notice carefully that with the word *providence* we do not refer to God the Lord himself, but to his work. Scripture is filled with teaching about that. For example, consider the picture given by the splendid Psalm 104: he causes the grass to grow for the livestock, and plants to grow for human beings to cultivate (v. 14); "O Lord, how manifold are your works!" (v. 24). God even calls the stars by name (Isa. 40:26). But he also cares for the birds of the air and the lilies of the field (Matt. 6:26,

28). Our breath is in God's hand (Pss. 76:12; 146:1–4; Acts 17:28). Spring and summer, fall and winter do not come automatically, but by virtue of God's promise to Noah (Gen. 8:22).

The Romans did not know that, and that is why they worshiped the goddess Fortuna, whose name means "fortune" or "luck." But Jesus said that apart from God not even one sparrow falls down from the roof, and the hairs on our head are known to him (Matt. 10:29–31; Luke 12:6–7). Therefore we should not play around with God's providence (for example, playing games of chance). If it is necessary that we cast lots, we should first seek God's blessing (Acts 1:26).

The pagan Greeks and Romans were for the most part fatalists, which means they worshiped fate. They thought that even Jupiter, the supreme deity, was unable to rescue someone from death.

Later, some Christians came to believe that God always looked far ahead to see what a person would do. This view was condemned by the Synod of Dort. All such foolish reasoning removes our heavenly Father from his throne (see Pss. 11:4; 93:2). As we saw earlier in Lord's Day 9, God makes everything happen according to his counsel (plan, forethought), but that execution of God's counsel far surpasses our understanding. God is great, and we do not comprehend him (Job 36:26): "For my thoughts are not your thoughts, neither are your ways my ways, declares the Lord" (Isa. 55:8). The sons of Jacob took counsel together extensively regarding what they would do with Joseph (Gen. 37), but afterward they appeared to have been fulfilling God's counsel, namely, God's plan to preserve a great nation (Gen. 45:5; 50:20). At first it appeared that Jesus was born in the town of Bethlehem simply on account of the commands of Caesar Augustus (Luke 2), but afterward people consulted the ancient prophecies where the birthplace of Bethlehem was mentioned directly (Matt. 2:1–6).

Q&A 28

Q. What does it benefit us to know that God has created all things and still upholds them by his providence?

A. We can be patient in adversity, thankful in prosperity, and with a view to the future we can have a firm confidence in our faithful God and Father that no creature shall separate us from his love; for all creatures are so completely in his hand that without his will they cannot so much as move.

Within that creation of God's mighty hand, things can happen about which we think, How is it possible? But let us never forget that it is God who assigns limits and boundaries (Job 1:12), and that nothing can separate us from his love (Rom. 8:32–39). Even the activities of the demons and the wicked must serve God's plans. We see this with our Savior, who was unjustly crucified by Jews and Gentiles. They were the ones who did it (John 19:11; Acts 2:23–24), but in this way the sacrifice of the Mediator was rendered for us.

But other things happen that cause us to rejoice. Every day the sun shines and the rain falls. They don't do this simply by themselves. Scripture calls them God's servants (Ps. 119:91). Our heavenly Father should be praised every day for our food and drink, clothes, dwelling, etc. (Deut. 8:10; Ps. 147:12; Jas. 4:15).

In adversity we should follow the example of Job, who said, "The LORD gave, and the LORD has taken away; blessed be the name of the LORD" (Job 1:21). When the disobedient people in the days of Amos refused to believe that they were being visited by God with adversity as punishment for their forsaking the covenant, the prophet said, "Does disaster come to a city, unless the LORD has done it?" (Amos 3:6).

Even the righteous are called to rejoice when they suffer for Jesus's sake (Acts 5:41; 1 Pet. 4:14). The Lord Jesus taught his disciples to view adversity on account of faith in him as the pruning of a vine (John 15). Initially Asaph, the composer of Psalm 73, was jealous about the prosperity of the wicked. But when he considered their end, he called himself a fool and promised improvement: I will hold faithfully to you and not depart from you again. He confessed, "You hold my right hand [as a father takes his son by the hand]. You guide me with your counsel, and afterward you will receive me to glory" (Ps. 73:23–24). If a person forthrightly confesses his sin, God will lead him, as though by the hand, through his Word and Spirit, and with his care will guide him out of the difficult position he was facing.

Scripture References

Psalm 147:1–20

> Praise the LORD!
> For it is good to sing praises to our God;
>> for it is pleasant, and a song of praise is fitting.
> The LORD builds up Jerusalem;
>> he gathers the outcasts of Israel.
> He heals the brokenhearted
>> and binds up their wounds.
> He determines the number of the stars;
>> he gives to all of them their names.
> Great is our Lord, and abundant in power;
>> his understanding is beyond measure.
> The LORD lifts up the humble;
>> he casts the wicked to the ground.
>
> Sing to the LORD with thanksgiving;
>> make melody to our God on the lyre!
> He covers the heavens with clouds;
>> he prepares rain for the earth;
>> he makes grass grow on the hills.
> He gives to the beasts their food,
>> and to the young ravens that cry.
> His delight is not in the strength of the horse,
>> nor his pleasure in the legs of a man,
> but the LORD takes pleasure in those who fear him,
>> in those who hope in his steadfast love.
>
> Praise the LORD, O Jerusalem!
>> Praise your God, O Zion!

For he strengthens the bars of your gates;
> he blesses your children within you.

He makes peace in your borders;
> he fills you with the finest of the wheat.

He sends out his command to the earth;
> his word runs swiftly.

He gives snow like wool;
> he scatters frost like ashes.

He hurls down his crystals of ice like crumbs;
> who can stand before his cold?

He sends out his word, and melts them;
> he makes his wind blow and the waters flow.

He declares his word to Jacob,
> his statutes and rules to Israel.

He has not dealt thus with any other nation;
> they do not know his rules.

Praise the Lord!

Isaiah 14:27

For the Lord of hosts has purposed,
> and who will annul it?

His hand is stretched out,
> and who will turn it back?

Isaiah 55:8–9

For my thoughts are not your thoughts,
> neither are your ways my ways, declares the Lord.

For as the heavens are higher than the earth,
> so are my ways higher than your ways
> and my thoughts than your thoughts."

Nehemiah 9:6

"You are the Lord, you alone. You have made heaven, the heaven of heavens, with all their host, the earth and all that is on it, the seas and all that is in them; and you preserve all of them; and the host of heaven worships you."

John 15:1–2

"I am the true vine, and my Father is the vinedresser. Every branch in me that does not bear fruit he takes away, and every branch that does bear fruit he prunes, that it may bear more fruit."

Acts 17:24–25

"The God who made the world and everything in it, being Lord of heaven and earth, does not live in temples made by man, nor is he served by human hands, as though he needed anything, since he himself gives to all mankind life and breath and everything."

LORD'S DAY 11

Q&A 29

Q. *Why is the Son of God called Jesus, that is, Savior?*

A. Because he saves us from all our sins, and because salvation is not to be sought or found in anyone else.

The first person who was given to know that our Savior would be called Jesus was Mary, his mother. The second who was also given to know that God would show grace to Mary so that she might be the mother of Messiah Jesus was Joseph, who was betrothed to Mary. When they spoke later with each other, it became apparent that the same name had been foretold to both of them by the angel. The baby that the Holy Spirit would cause to be born of Mary would be called Joshua. We know that name from the Hebrew Old Testament, where it means "Yahweh bestows salvation." In the New Testament that name was rendered in Greek as Jesus.

Here two things are being confessed about this Jesus. First, he is our complete Savior, and second, he is our only Savior.

1. *Our complete Savior.* The angel told Joseph why the child of Mary would have the name Jesus, "For he will save his people from their sins" (Matt. 1:21). So it happened that when he was eight days old and was circumcised, the Savior was named Jesus (Luke 1:31). He continues to bear that name. He spoke from heaven to Paul as the latter was traveling to Damascus: "I am Jesus, whom you are persecuting" (Acts 9:5). We should speak

often about him and honor him, for he is worthy of that. For he has loved us and washed us from our sins in his blood (Rev. 1:5; 5:9). His blood cleanses us from all sin (1 John 1:7).

2. *Our only Savior.* Scripture knows of no peers for Jesus, whether men or women. Shortly after Jesus's ascension Peter explained to the Jewish council that this Jesus was the Stone they had put to death, and "there is salvation in no one else, for there is no other name under heaven given among men by which we must be saved" (Acts 4:12). As Paul wrote later: "For there is one God, and there is one mediator between God and men, the man Christ Jesus" (1 Tim. 2:5).

Q&A 30

Q. *Do those who seek their salvation or well-being in saints, in themselves, or anywhere else, also believe in the only Savior Jesus?*

A. No. Though they boast of him in words, they in fact deny the only Savior Jesus. For one of two things must be true: either Jesus is not a complete Savior, or those who by true faith accept this Savior must find in him all that is necessary for their salvation.

Unfortunately, disunity arose quickly with regard to Jesus's status as Savior. Christians of Jewish descent came and demanded of everyone, including Gentile converts, that unless they were circumcised according to the law of Moses, they could not be saved (Acts 15:1). These Jewish people were not holding to Jesus's own statement that he had come precisely to fulfill the law with all of its shadows (Matt. 5:17; 26:56; Luke 24:25, 44). God had shown Peter in a vision that the shadow-filled laws had passed away (for example, regarding eating pork; Acts 10). Those Jewish Christians did not think that believing in the Lord Jesus was sufficient. They turned the matter into a mathematical equation: the righteousness of the law *plus* the righteousness of Christ together were required as sufficient.

This heresy, known as Judaizing, was condemned by the apostles (Acts 15), and by Paul in his epistles to the Galatians and to the Romans.

Therefore here in Lord's Day 11 the church condemns the Roman Catholic version of Judaizing very severely. Roman Catholic teaching also construes the mediatorial work of Christ and the so-called good works of believers in terms of a mathematical equation. There have never been so-called saints who performed an overabundance of good works, which supposedly constitute "the treasury of merit," whereby the "spiritual" would be able to assist others by means of letters of indulgence. Such superstition, which brings Christians once again under a yoke, is not consistent with Scripture (Col. 2:8, 16; Gal. 5:1).

Every attempt to establish conditions that we would first have to satisfy before we can believe that we are children of Abraham or children of our heavenly Father—for example, that one must first have a conversion experience—also sounds as somber and serious as that Judaizing talk, but it is all a devilishly dangerous attempt to make covenant children into slaves again. Everyone can simply abandon himself or herself to the promises of God's covenant, as long as he or she desires salvation and redemption exclusively from Jesus, and not one bit from oneself.

Scripture References

Matthew 1:21
"She will bear a son, and you shall call his name Jesus, for he will save his people from their sins."

Acts 4:12
"And there is salvation in no one else, for there is no other name under heaven given among men by which we must be saved."

Galatians 2:21
I do not nullify the grace of God, for if righteousness were through the law, then Christ died for no purpose.

Galatians 5:1
For freedom Christ has set us free; stand firm therefore, and do not submit again to a yoke of slavery.

Galatians 5:4
You are severed from Christ, you who would be justified by the law; you have fallen away from grace.

Hebrews 5:9
And being made perfect, he became the source of eternal salvation to all who obey him.

LORD'S DAY 12

Q&A 31

Q. *Why is he called Christ, that is, Anointed?*

A. Because he has been ordained by God the Father, and anointed with the Holy Spirit, to be our chief Prophet and Teacher, who has fully revealed to us the secret counsel and will of God concerning our redemption; our only High Priest, who by the one sacrifice of his body has redeemed us, and who continually intercedes for us before the Father; and our eternal King, who governs us by his Word and Spirit, and who defends and preserves us in the redemption obtained for us.

The name Jesus is comparable to our names John and Mary, as proper names, but the name Christ is comparable to titles like baker, mayor, and the like. Most often we place the name Jesus first and speak of "Jesus Christ" or of "Jesus the Christ." By way of exception we speak of "Christ Jesus," in which his work title comes first.

For in Israel, people did not simply take for themselves titles like prophet, priest, and the like. People had to be called to that (Heb. 5:4), and as a sign of one's orderly appointment, one was anointed with oil (Lev. 8:12, Aaron; 1 Sam. 10:1; 16:13; 1 Kgs. 1:39, Saul, David, and Solomon).

Oil was indispensable, since it was used for preparing spices, dressing wounds, and fueling lamps. Father Jacob carried a little vessel of oil with him for keeping his feet soft on the hot ground. Guests were received with aromatic oil. No wonder that on account of its nourishing, illuminating, healing, and reviving powers, Scripture uses oil as a picture of the Holy Spirit (1 Sam. 10:6; 16:13).

Anointing points to two realities. First, to calling, and second, to equipping. The anointing of the Lord Jesus at his baptism in the Jordan occurred through the Holy Spirit himself. That Spirit descended upon him in bodily form, like a dove. First our Savior was appointed publicly as Mediator. He was no usurper. Here the word *ordained* means "appointed" (Heb. 3:1–2; 5:4–5). But in the second place, the term *christos* means that our Savior was also equipped for fulfilling his office. Already in Isaiah 61:1 we read the words of the future Messiah, "The Spirit of the Lord God is upon me," and when Jesus read these words in the synagogue of Nazareth, he said, "Today this Scripture has been fulfilled in your hearing" (Luke 4:21).

Jesus was appointed and equipped for a threefold task, namely, to the office of prophet, priest, and king. We turn to that now.

1. *The prophetic office of our Savior.* Some people think that a prophet is someone who predicts the future. That is incorrect, for a prophet is someone who speaks the Word of God, a teacher of Scripture, and this phenomenon extends to the past, the present, and the future. God had sent such prophets already to his ancient church, namely, to Israel (1 Pet. 1:12). But when Jesus came, he clearly surpassed every preceding prophet. "But I say to you" (Matt. 5:28) was his refrain. He never said, "Thus says Yahweh," for he himself had authority to speak and to teach (Matt. 7:29). Later the apostles could prophesy only because of the Spirit of Christ (John 16:13; 1 Pet. 1:12). At that point everything necessary for our salvation was revealed (John 17:3; Heb. 1:1). Therefore it is ingratitude toward Scripture as the Word of God given through prophets and apostles to dare to think we need to add anything. For that reason it is actually forbidden to call anyone in the church "father" (Matt. 23:9).

2. *The priestly office of our Savior.* The church goes on to confess in her Catechism that our Lord was appointed and anointed to be "our only High Priest, who by the one sacrifice of his body

has redeemed us, and who continually intercedes for us before the Father."

In ancient times God gave his people priests. These priests brought sacrifices, blessed the people, taught the people, and so on. But all those shadows are fulfilled by the coming of Christ. Christ's high-priesthood was unique in that he did not inherit it from his father, as did the descendants of Aaron. He was a priest after the order of Melchizedek, which means that he became priest not through inheritance but through appointment. Christ's sacrifice was also unrepeatable, once for all time (Heb. 7:27). And the holy of holies, where he entered, was the heavenly glory (Heb. 9:12, 24), and he continues there as our Advocate (Rom. 5:9–10; 8:34; Heb. 7:25; 9:24). Our Savior gave himself as a ransom in order to purchase our freedom (Mark 10:45). It is insulting to claim that Christ's sacrifice on the cross is repeated when the mass is administered. Moreover, to talk of "priests" performing that mass is also a serious mistake.

3. *The kingly office of our Lord Jesus.* Thirdly, we confess Christ also as our eternal King, "who governs us by his Word and Spirit, and who defends and preserves us in the redemption obtained for us."

Notice how God resented it when Israel wanted to have a king lead the way in times of war against her enemies (1 Sam. 8). Israel's kings, like David and others, had to be strengthened by the Holy Spirit, and Israel had to expect the Messiah as the highest king. But when Christ came, the majority of the leaders and the people were initially amazed at Jesus's miracles and at times wanted to declare him king (John 6:15). But when Jesus talked about a suffering Messiah, many people wanted nothing more to do with him.

"My kingdom is not of this world," Jesus told Pilate. His kingdom would not expand with weapons of iron, but with the sword of the Spirit, which is God's Word (Eph. 6:17). Christ was appointed as king over Zion, his church (Ps. 2:6). He is her Head (Eph. 1:22). One day the kingdom of Christ will defeat every dominion of flesh, and the prophecy of the stone in the dream of Nebuchadnezzer will be fulfilled in reality (Dan. 2:34, 44). Let no one exercise dominion over the flock of Jesus, the Chief Shepherd of the sheep (Matt. 20:25–28; Heb. 13:20; 1 Pet. 5:2–3).

Q&A 32

Q. *Why are you called a Christian?*

A. Because I am a member of Christ by faith and thus share in his anointing, so that I may as prophet confess his name, as priest present myself a living sacrifice of thankfulness to him, and as king fight with a free and good conscience against sin and the devil in this life, and hereafter reign with him eternally over all creatures.

Just as the Lord Jesus was anointed by the Holy Spirit at his baptism in the Jordan, so too later his disciples received the Holy Spirit. Both Jesus's promise shortly before his ascension ("John baptized with water, but you will be baptized with the Holy Spirit," Acts 1:5; 11:16; see John 14:26) and other promises given in the old dispensation in Joel 2:28–32 were fulfilled in Jerusalem, on the famous day of Pentecost. The Spirit descended not only upon the disciples but also upon ordinary people ("all flesh") in the church. The Spirit descended later even upon Gentiles like Cornelius (Acts 10–11). It is true, the flood of the extraordinary gifts of the Spirit has ceased, whereby in the early days so many miracles occurred, like casting out evil spirits, speaking in new tongues, and healing sick people (Mark 16:17–18), but through the formation of the New Testament many have been converted to the Christian faith.

Here the church is confessing that all who believe in Christ are called to the following threefold task.

1. *To our prophetic task.* The Catechism draws our attention to this with the words "so that I may as prophet confess his name." For that, Bible knowledge is needed. We must not be ashamed of Christ's name, but we must mention it now and then. In short: hearing and reading and doing God's Word—that is prophesying today. That is not exclusively the work of the minister and elders, but of all church members, old and young. In the fight

against false teachers, John appealed to the knowledge of the Word among the entire church (1 John 2).

2. *To our priestly task.* When faith in Christ ends up costing us, then we must willingly bear those costs (Col. 1:24; 1 Pet. 4:16; Phil. 2:17). This includes persecution. We must pray for our persecutors, just as Jesus and Stephen did.

3. *To our kingly task.* Whoever persists in sin is a slave of sin (John 8:34). At that point the devil is our master. But whoever believes in Christ does not yield entrance to sin and the devil, otherwise our conscience would again be loaded down with guilt (Rom. 6:12; 1 Tim. 1:18–19). We must fight not with fleshly instruments but with instruments of the Spirit, in view of the description of the armor of the church in Ephesians 6:10–20.

Scripture References

Luke 1:32–33
"He will be great and will be called the Son of the Most High. And the Lord God will give to him the throne of his father David, and he will reign over the house of Jacob forever, and of his kingdom there will be no end."

Luke 4:16–21
And he came to Nazareth, where he had been brought up. And as was his custom, he went to the synagogue on the Sabbath day, and he stood up to read. And the scroll of the prophet Isaiah was given to him. He unrolled the scroll and found the place where it was written,

> "The Spirit of the Lord is upon me,
>   because he has anointed me
>   to proclaim good news to the poor.
> He has sent me to proclaim liberty to the captives
>   and recovering of sight to the blind,
>   to set at liberty those who are oppressed,
> to proclaim the year of the Lord's favor."

And he rolled up the scroll and gave it back to the attendant and sat down. And the eyes of all in the synagogue were fixed on him. And he began to say to them, "Today this Scripture has been fulfilled in your hearing."

Acts 3:22
Moses said, "The Lord God will raise up for you a prophet like me from your brothers. You shall listen to him in whatever he tells you."

Hebrews 3:1
Therefore, holy brothers, you who share in a heavenly calling, consider Jesus, the apostle and high priest of our confession.

Hebrews 5:4-5
And no one takes this honor for himself, but only when called by God, just as Aaron was. So also Christ did not exalt himself to be made a high priest, but was appointed by him who said to him,

> "You are my Son,
>   today I have begotten you."

LORD'S DAY 13

Q&A 33

Q. *Why is he called God's only begotten Son, since we also are children of God?*

A. Because Christ alone is the eternal, natural Son of God. We, however, are children of God by adoption, through grace, for Christ's sake.

The elderly Elizabeth, the mother of John the Baptist, was one of the first whom God told that Mary would become the mother of God's Son (Luke 1:35, 43). Jesus was six months younger than John. Nevertheless John once said: "He [Jesus] was before me" (John 1:30). One time Jesus himself said: "Before Abraham was, I am" (John 8:58). There are more such passages.

But how could that be?

That could be because Christ was not only a real baby and a real man but also the Son of God who was eternally with the Father and was himself also God, and thus was Creator of heaven and earth. To be sure, during his stay on earth he did not regularly demonstrate this; only occasionally did he do so. In light of this, the apostle Paul wrote that Christ never used his power to serve himself (Phil. 2:6–8; Rom. 15:3), but only until his resurrection, for at that point he proved that he was the Son of God. Finally, when standing before Caiaphas, Jesus did not need to remain silent any longer and confessed that he was God's Son (Matt. 26:63–64).

Church history informs us that repeatedly there were numbers of people who thought that Jesus was not really God. In connection with Lord's Day 8, we discussed Arius. This heretic claimed that God had created the Lord Jesus beforehand, before the creation. Later on there were heretics who claimed that Christ became God for the first time after his death and resurrection.

In contradiction of all those errors, we read, for example, what the apostle John writes, that Christ was there in the beginning (that is, with the creation; John 1:1), and he later informs us concerning Jesus that he was a real man, from whose dead corpse blood and water flowed (John 19:34).

Here the church confesses correctly that God's Son was not created and was not promoted to be God's Son, but that he is God of God, of the same nature as his Father. For Scripture calls him the only begotten Son (see John 3:16; 1 John 4:9 KJV), who is God's own Son (Rom. 8:32). Scripture also says that anyone who denies the Son denies the Father as well (1 John 2:23).

Christ was God, which is why his shedding of blood was of such great power and value (1 John 1:7).

But now we should mention something else. In Scripture we too are called "sons and daughters" of God (2 Cor. 6:18). But that is not the same.

First, the Lord Jesus is eternally completely God, but people are only creatures. Humanity (in Adam) conducted itself unbecomingly, by not being satisfied with the honor of having been created in God's image (Gen. 1:26–27), when Satan showed the way in which (in his opinion) humanity could be its own boss. This was terrible (Gen. 3:4–6). It is indeed proof that God is very gracious, and that by bringing the Word of truth within the heart of this deeply fallen humanity, he thereby instilled faith and renewed such people in his image (Col. 3:10; Jas. 1:18), so that in everything as obedient children they again desire to obey the will of their heavenly Father (Mark 3:33–35). This is called being "born of God" (1 John 3:9), but not in such a way that believing people are equal with God. Our Savior alone is God's only begotten Son, eternally equal to the Father and one with the Father.

Furthermore, our Savior had every right to assert himself as the Son of God, but we have become able to call him Father thanks to God's grace.

Let us also remember that we obtained a share in this grace apart from being Jews. You need only to study history. God did indeed want to have a covenant of grace with Israel (at Horeb, for the sake of Abraham). But our ancestors were lifelong pagans. Now for the first time, since "the dividing wall of hostility" has been broken down (Eph. 2:14) and "the record of debt that stood against us with its legal demands" has been cancelled (Col. 2:14), we and our children also have the right to call God Father (Gal. 3:26).

Q&A 34

Q. Why do you call him our Lord?

A. Because he has ransomed us, body and soul, from all our sins, not with silver or gold but with his precious blood, and has freed us from all the power of the devil to make us his own possession.

We need not hesitate at all when Scripture uses words like *masters* and *slaves*. Jesus is such a good Master for us, since he gave his life for us on the cross.

Some Bible translations print the name LORD (in small capitals) as a translation of the Hebrew of God's name, Yahweh. Nowadays people also replace that with "Lord" (referring to God). But because our Savior, who was Mediator between God and people, is called *Kyrios* in the Greek, he is often called "the Lord Jesus." *Kyrios* was used as an exalted title, for example, for the Roman emperor, but one could also use it in reference to the owner of a vineyard (Mark 12:9), over which his care extended, or one whose care extended to a dog (Matt. 15:27) or to a female slave (Acts 16:16) or a male slave (Eph. 6:5).

Frequently our Savior was called *Kyrios* (Lord) not because he was God—which of course was the case—but because he was really man and as such obeyed to the point of death the mediatorial task that called upon him to undergo death; then, however,

he arose from the grave and could say, "All authority in heaven
and earth has been given to me" (Matt. 28:18; see Rom. 14:9).
Behind the idea of exercising dominion stands the Greek phrase
that means "to be *kyrios*." This was not a nasty expression. God
has taken pity upon the entire human race and desires the gospel
of life to be preached to all people (Matt. 28:19–20).

Scripture References

Romans 9:5
To them belong the patriarchs, and from their race, according to the flesh,
is the Christ, who is God over all, blessed forever. Amen.

Romans 8:15
For you did not receive the spirit of slavery to fall back into fear, but you
have received the Spirit of adoption as sons, by whom we cry, "Abba! Father!"

Romans 14:1–15:13
As for the one who is weak in faith, welcome him, but not to quarrel over
opinions. One person believes he may eat anything, while the weak person eats only vegetables. Let not the one who eats despise the one who
abstains, and let not the one who abstains pass judgment on the one who
eats, for God has welcomed him. Who are you to pass judgment on the
servant of another? It is before his own master that he stands or falls. And
he will be upheld, for the Lord is able to make him stand.

One person esteems one day as better than another, while another esteems all days alike. Each one should be fully convinced in his own mind.
The one who observes the day, observes it in honor of the Lord. The one
who eats, eats in honor of the Lord, since he gives thanks to God, while the
one who abstains, abstains in honor of the Lord and gives thanks to God.
For none of us lives to himself, and none of us dies to himself. For if we
live, we live to the Lord, and if we die, we die to the Lord. So then, whether
we live or whether we die, we are the Lord's. For to this end Christ died
and lived again, that he might be Lord both of the dead and of the living.

Why do you pass judgment on your brother? Or you, why do you despise your brother? For we will all stand before the judgment seat of God;
for it is written,

"As I live, says the Lord, every knee shall bow to me,
    and every tongue shall confess to God."

So then each of us will give an account of himself to God.

Therefore let us not pass judgment on one another any longer, but rather decide never to put a stumbling block or hindrance in the way of a brother. I know and am persuaded in the Lord Jesus that nothing is unclean in itself, but it is unclean for anyone who thinks it unclean. For if your brother is grieved by what you eat, you are no longer walking in love. By what you eat, do not destroy the one for whom Christ died. So do not let what you regard as good be spoken of as evil. For the kingdom of God is not a matter of eating and drinking but of righteousness and peace and joy in the Holy Spirit. Whoever thus serves Christ is acceptable to God and approved by men. So then let us pursue what makes for peace and for mutual upbuilding.

Do not, for the sake of food, destroy the work of God. Everything is indeed clean, but it is wrong for anyone to make another stumble by what he eats. It is good not to eat meat or drink wine or do anything that causes your brother to stumble. The faith that you have, keep between yourself and God. Blessed is the one who has no reason to pass judgment on himself for what he approves. But whoever has doubts is condemned if he eats, because the eating is not from faith. For whatever does not proceed from faith is sin.

We who are strong have an obligation to bear with the failings of the weak, and not to please ourselves. Let each of us please his neighbor for his good, to build him up. For Christ did not please himself, but as it is written, 'The reproaches of those who reproached you fell on me.' For whatever was written in former days was written for our instruction, that through endurance and through the encouragement of the Scriptures we might have hope. May the God of endurance and encouragement grant you to live in such harmony with one another, in accord with Christ Jesus, that together you may with one voice glorify the God and Father of our Lord Jesus Christ. Therefore welcome one another as Christ has welcomed you, for the glory of God.

For I tell you that Christ became a servant to the circumcised to show God's truthfulness, in order to confirm the promises given to the patriarchs, and in order that the Gentiles might glorify God for his mercy. As it is written,

"Therefore I will praise you among the Gentiles,
    and sing to your name."

And again it is said,

> "Rejoice, O Gentiles, with his people."

And again,

> "Praise the Lord, all you Gentiles,
>   and let all the peoples extol him."

And again Isaiah says,

> "The root of Jesse will come,
>   even he who arises to rule the Gentiles;
> in him will the Gentiles hope."

May the God of hope fill you with all joy and peace in believing, so that by the power of the Holy Spirit you may abound in hope.

1 Corinthians 6:18
Flee from sexual immorality. Every other sin a person commits is outside the body, but the sexually immoral person sins against his own body.

1 Corinthians 7:23
You were bought with a price; do not become bondservants of men.

Philippians 2:5–6
Have this mind among yourselves, which is yours in Christ Jesus, who, though he was in the form of God, did not count equality with God a thing to be grasped.

LORD'S DAY 14

Q&A 35

Q. *What do you confess when you say: He was conceived by the Holy Spirit, born of the virgin Mary?*

A. The eternal Son of God, who is and remains true and eternal God, took upon himself true human nature from the flesh and blood of the virgin Mary, through the working of the Holy Spirit. Thus he is also the true seed of David, and like his brothers in every respect, yet without sin.

If you want to read something brief and clear about the conception and birth of Christ, you will find that in the early chapters of Matthew and Luke. Elsewhere these subjects are described somewhat differently, in greater depth, because those who opposed these teachings were themselves being opposed by those biblical writers. Some were saying that God's Son did not really become man, did not really suffer, die, rise, and go to heaven, but that all of this merely *appeared* to happen. For this reason, these false teachers were called Docetists (according to the Greek word *dokeō*, "to seem, to appear"). We are warned against them especially by the apostle John, both in his epistles as well as in his Gospel.

The apostle John has certainly contended against this false teaching in his three epistles. There he writes that he himself had seen the Lord Jesus (1 John 1:1–4), that we cannot be saved apart from the shedding of his blood, and that we must renounce all sin and iniquity (1 John 1:5–10). The apostle writes, "Every spirit that confesses that Jesus Christ has come in the flesh is from God, and every spirit that does not confess Jesus is not from God. This is the spirit of the antichrist, which you heard was coming and now is in the world already" (1 John 4:2–3).

But it is in his Gospel that John contends most powerfully against those who denied Christ's real deity and true humanity. In his introduction to this book (John 1:1–18), John asserts the deity of Christ immediately at the beginning: "In the beginning was the Word, and the Word was with God, and the Word was God" (John 1:1). This *Logos* (the Greek word for "Word") possessed the honor of being Creator of all things (1:3, 4, 10). Nevertheless this Logos was not honored and acknowledged when he came to earth as a man. Recall how scandalously his predecessor, John the Baptist, was opposed.

Following this introduction (1:1–18), John narrates a number of facts—several of which only John tells us—merely to prove that the Son of God became true man. Subsequently God's Son lived a life in which he not only endured exhaustion, hunger, and thirst, but also was crucified, died, and was buried. For he was truly dead, as we see when a soldier pierced Jesus's side with a spear, and blood and water flowed from the wound. This proved that he was really dead (John 19:34)! Later various people received genuine proof that this same Jesus arose and went to heaven.

The entire New Testament is in agreement on this.

Just like us, our Savior had a mother who brought him into this world and gave him birth (Luke 2:6–7). In the Gospel of John she is never called by her name, Mary, but is identified only as the mother of Jesus.

But what preceded his birth was different than with us. With each of us, God our Father made use of the marriage of our parents in order to bring about the birth of a baby from our mother, who brought us into the world in God's time.

But our Savior was not conceived by Mary in this way. For with this event, God made no use of the functions of marriage. Joseph learned for the first time through an angel about the conception of Christ by Mary (Matt. 1:18–20). Our Savior was conceived by his mother apart from the ordinary functions of marriage. That was specifically and exclusively the work of the Holy Spirit, as we learn from the words of the angel spoken to Mary: "The Holy Spirit will come upon you, and the power of the Most High will overshadow you" (Luke 1:35).

Q&A 36

Q. *What benefit do you receive from the holy conception and birth of Christ?*

A. He is our Mediator, and with his innocence and perfect holiness covers, in the sight of God, my sin, in which I was conceived and born.

So God's Son took on our flesh and blood from the virgin Mary (Luke 1:31–32). The apostle John states it briefly: "The Word became flesh" (John 1:14).

But during his stay on earth, Jesus never once made use of this uniquely exalted position for his own benefit (Rom. 15:3). In light of this, Paul once wrote, "For there is one God, and there is one mediator between God and men, the man Christ Jesus, who gave himself as a ransom for all, which is the testimony given at the proper time" (1 Tim. 2:5–6). As Isaiah prophesied,

> He was oppressed, and he was afflicted,
>   yet he opened not his mouth;
> like a lamb that is led to the slaughter,
>   and like a sheep that before its shearers is silent,
>   so he opened not his mouth. (Isa. 53:7)

Read as well the apostles Peter and Jude regarding Jesus as the Lamb.

Scripture References

Matthew 1:18
Now the birth of Jesus Christ took place in this way. When his mother Mary had been betrothed to Joseph, before they came together she was found to be with child from the Holy Spirit.

Luke 1:35
And the angel answered her, "The Holy Spirit will come upon you, and the power of the Most High will overshadow you; therefore the child to be born will be called holy—the Son of God."

John 1:29
The next day he saw Jesus coming toward him, and said, "Behold, the Lamb of God, who takes away the sin of the world!"

Acts 20:28-30
"Pay careful attention to yourselves and to all the flock, in which the Holy Spirit has made you overseers, to care for the church of God, which he obtained with his own blood. I know that after my departure fierce wolves will come in among you, not sparing the flock; and from among your own selves will arise men speaking twisted things, to draw away the disciples after them."

2 Peter 3:18
But grow in the grace and knowledge of our Lord and Savior Jesus Christ. To him be the glory both now and to the day of eternity. Amen.

Jude 19
It is these who cause divisions, worldly people, devoid of the Spirit.

LORD'S DAY 15

Q&A 37

Q. *What do you confess when you say that he suffered?*

A. During all the time he lived on earth, but especially at the end, Christ bore in body and soul the wrath of God against the sin of the whole human race. Thus, by his suffering, as the only atoning sacrifice, he has redeemed our body and soul from everlasting damnation, and obtained for us the grace of God, righteousness, and eternal life.

"During all the time he lived on earth." That was thirty-three years. That's how long Christ lived on earth. He entered the world in poverty (Luke 2:7). Joseph and Mary had to flee with him to Egypt in fear of King Herod (Matt. 2:13). Christ was tempted for forty days by the devil (Matt. 4:1–11). He suffered intensely in the garden of Gethsemane. After a frightening night he was led before Caiaphas and sentenced to death. Pilate did not oppose his crucifixion. Christ complained that even God had forsaken him (Matt. 27:46). In this way he bore the heavy burden of God's wrath against the sins of humanity. Only on the basis of the obedience of the second Adam (Christ) is God willing to interact with the world of humanity.

Q&A 38

Q. *Why did he suffer under Pontius Pilate as judge?*

A. Though innocent, Christ was condemned by an earthly judge, and so he freed us from the severe judgment of God that was to fall on us

---

The Catechism says that Christ suffered under Pontius Pilate, and that is true, but it could better have said that Christ suffered under Caiaphas. Pontius Pilate faced the Lord Jesus because the Sanhedrin, the Jewish council, was itself not allowed to execute Jesus (Luke 23; John 19). No fewer than five times Pilate explicitly declared that he found the Lord Jesus innocent. He was afraid for his own skin. The Jews could have brought accusation against him to the emperor (John 19:12). On Pentecost Peter explained the matter (Acts 2:14–40).

Q&A 39

Q. *Does it have a special meaning that Christ was crucified and did not die in a different way?*

A. Yes. Thereby I am assured that he took upon himself the curse which lay on me, for a crucified one was cursed by God.

When the Lord Jesus performed so many miracles, that activity made a huge impression. For example, after the multiplication of the loaves, the crowd wanted to take him along to Jerusalem to proclaim him as king (John 6:14–15). Since the Savior was not prepared to accommodate that, many turned away from him. When he ended up before the Sanhedrin, the Jewish leaders found him to be a danger to their people and to their own position, because the Romans would have intervened (John 11:48). Nevertheless, during the hearing before the Jewish council, Jesus declared forthrightly that he was the Messiah, the Christ. Consequently, in terms of Jewish thought Jesus was a rebel against

Roman authority, and the Romans had the fixed rule that rebels against the emperor were to be punished with crucifixion. Later the Jews were continually offended by the preaching of the apostles of a gospel that proclaimed the crucified Messiah (1 Cor. 1:23). Indeed, in the ancient Torah we read in Deuteronomy 21:23 that one who was hanged was accursed by God.

Scripture Reference

Isaiah 53:1–12

Who has believed what he has heard from us?
  And to whom has the arm of the LORD been revealed?
For he grew up before him like a young plant,
  and like a root out of dry ground;
he had no form or majesty that we should look at him,
  and no beauty that we should desire him.
He was despised and rejected by men;
  a man of sorrows, and acquainted with grief;
and as one from whom men hide their faces
  he was despised, and we esteemed him not.

Surely he has borne our griefs
  and carried our sorrows;
yet we esteemed him stricken,
  smitten by God, and afflicted.
But he was pierced for our transgressions;
  he was crushed for our iniquities;
upon him was the chastisement that brought us peace,
  and with his wounds we are healed.
All we like sheep have gone astray;
  we have turned—every one—to his own way;
and the LORD has laid on him
  the iniquity of us all.

He was oppressed, and he was afflicted,
  yet he opened not his mouth;
like a lamb that is led to the slaughter,
  and like a sheep that before its shearers is silent,
  so he opened not his mouth.

By oppression and judgment he was taken away;
    and as for his generation, who considered
that he was cut off out of the land of the living,
    stricken for the transgression of my people?
And they made his grave with the wicked
    and with a rich man in his death,
although he had done no violence,
    and there was no deceit in his mouth.

Yet it was the will of the Lord to crush him;
    he has put him to grief;
when his soul makes an offering for guilt,
    he shall see his offspring; he shall prolong his days;
the will of the Lord shall prosper in his hand.
Out of the anguish of his soul he shall see and be satisfied;
by his knowledge shall the righteous one, my servant,
    make many to be accounted righteous,
    and he shall bear their iniquities.
Therefore I will divide him a portion with the many,
    and he shall divide the spoil with the strong,
because he poured out his soul to death
    and was numbered with the transgressors;
yet he bore the sin of many,
    and makes intercession for the transgressors.

LORD'S DAY 16

God's "justice and truth" were discussed earlier in connection with Lord's Days 4, 5, and 6.

In the first place, by his disobedience Adam plunged himself and all his descendants into ruin (Rom. 2:19; 5:12; 6:23). "In this the love of God was made manifest among us, that God sent his only Son into the world," so that everyone who "believes in him should not perish but have eternal life" (1 John 4:9; John 3:16). Thus God's justice was satisfied by the death of our Savior.

Secondly, almost immediately after Adam's disastrous fall, God gave the promise that he would save us from the powers of Satan (Gen. 3:15) and thereby from the power of death (Heb. 2:14). The entire Old Testament was flavored by that glorious promise. For example, recall that the slaughter of the Passover lamb at twilight (or as the Hebrew says, "between the two evenings," that is, between four o'clock and six o'clock, Exod. 12:6) was fulfilled on Golgotha (John 19:14; Luke 23:54; see also Heb. 13:11–12). The entire Old Testament was moving toward Christ's death. When that death occurred, God's truth (that is, his faithfulness) was evident.

Q&A 41

Q. *Why was he buried?*

A. His burial testified that he had really died.

The Romans did not proceed tenderly when implementing crucifixion. They often rendered the victim helpless by breaking his bones, because occasionally victims would be taken from the cross by their followers and thus rescued from death. With broken bones the criminals, if kept alive, would be rendered helpless for the rest of their lives. What happened to those men crucified along with Jesus? We don't know. Perhaps their bodies were disposed of or burned.

But Jesus was buried. That first of all.

Secondly, Jesus received a rich man's grave. Nicodemus and Joseph of Arimathea fulfilled Isaiah 53:9 by providing Jesus a grave in the side of a rock, and wrapped his body in cloths that had been scented with myrrh and aloe, with coverings for head and body.

Q&A 42

Q. *Since Christ has died for us, why do we still have to die?*

A. Our death is not a payment for our sins, but it puts an end to sin and is an entrance into eternal life.

It is indeed appointed to man to die once (Heb. 9:27). All people must die. But because the death of believers is a transition to eternal life, the question arises whether it is actually fair for God to allow believers to die. After all, Jesus bore the punishment for them. Why must they still die?

We would answer this question by saying, first, that in the life of believers there unfortunately remains all too much that is hardly sinless and perfect. We continue to be children of Adam, surely in terms of our old nature. We must still "go the way of all the earth" (as David calls dying in 1 Kgs. 2:2).

But in the second place, we would point out that our death is not retribution, but already in this life God prunes the branches of the Vine who is Christ by means of adversity and suffering (John 15). Only when we've died does sin cease (Rom. 6:7; 1 Pet. 4:1). We cannot enter eternal life as we are now. Mortality cannot inherit immortality. Even the believers who will experience the day of Jesus's return still will have to be "changed" as well (1 Cor. 15:42, 50–51).

Q&A 43

Q. What further benefit do we receive from Christ's sacrifice and death on the cross?

A. Through Christ's death our old nature is crucified, put to death, and buried with him, so that the evil desires of the flesh may no longer reign in us, but that we may offer ourselves to him as a sacrifice of thankfulness.

The question asks, "What *further* benefit do we receive?"

For we have discussed more than once the forgiveness of our sins. But we must discuss as well the leaving behind of our sins. We are enabled to do that by Christ's Spirit. That Spirit provided us with the Bible, God's Word. This Word must be taught to us from our youth, in our parents' home, in the Christian school, and through the official preaching on the Christian day of rest. This is how we become more intimately connected as branches of Christ, the True Vine (John 15). Paul often calls this "being in Christ" (e.g., Rom. 6). Consider your baptism. Can such baptized people simply go on with sinful living? Of course not.

> How can we who died to sin still live in it? Do you not know that all of us who have been baptized into Christ Jesus were baptized into his death? We were buried therefore with him by baptism into death, in order that, just as Christ was raised from the dead by the glory of the Father, we too might walk in newness of life. For if we have been united with him in a death like his, we shall certainly be

united with him in a resurrection like his. We know that our old self was crucified with him in order that the body of sin might be brought to nothing, so that we would no longer be enslaved to sin. (Rom. 6:2–6)

Peter gave the same instruction to the Christians in Asia Minor (1 Pet. 1–4).

Putting to death our old nature, our old man, the earthly members of our body of sin, our flesh, all the sin that still dwells within us (all of these expressions refer to one and the same thing) can occur thanks to the suffering on the cross of our Lord Jesus and because the Spirit has united us with him through faith. Therefore Paul says, "I appeal to you therefore, brothers, by the mercies of God, [evident in the sending and in the death of Christ] to present your bodies as a living sacrifice, holy and acceptable to God, which is your spiritual worship" (Rom. 12:1).

Q&A 44

Q. *Why is there added: He descended into hell?*

A. In my greatest sorrows and temptations I may be assured and comforted that my Lord Jesus Christ, by his unspeakable anguish, pain, terror, and agony, which he endured throughout all his sufferings but especially on the cross, has delivered me from the anguish and torment of hell.

Formerly the word *hell* had a number of meanings, including first, the grave, and second, the place of the damned. Today people use the word *hell* exclusively in the second sense. Nevertheless, as a result of earlier usage the misunderstanding could arise that in the time between Jesus's burial and resurrection he was in the place of damnation. But Holy Scripture nowhere mentions that.

Our Savior did indeed undergo that damnation, but that occurred during his life here on earth. How distressed he was when he saw it approaching! He said, "Now is my soul troubled. And what shall I say? 'Father, save me from this hour'? But for this purpose I have come to this hour" (John 12:27). In the night before his death the "power of darkness" came upon him (Luke 22:53). The disciples were supposed to pray especially for protection from "temptation" (Luke 22:40). At that time Jesus even asked God to remove the cup of suffering from him. His sweat fell to the ground like great drops of blood (Luke 22:44). And on the cross, when it became dark, the Savior cried out, "My God, my God, why have you forsaken me?" (Matt. 27:46).

See how Christ has carried all our punishment. Therefore we may always call upon him, even when we don't know where to go with our accusing conscience. We may then call to God on the basis of Jesus's work, whose work as our security is completed. He was forsaken by God so that we might never be (Rom. 8:1, 34).

Scripture Reference

Psalm 22:1–31

> My God, my God, why have you forsaken me?
> > Why are you so far from saving me, from the words of my
> > > groaning?
> O my God, I cry by day, but you do not answer,
> > and by night, but I find no rest.
>
> Yet you are holy,
> > enthroned on the praises of Israel.
> In you our fathers trusted;
> > they trusted, and you delivered them.
> To you they cried and were rescued;
> > in you they trusted and were not put to shame.
>
> But I am a worm and not a man,
> > scorned by mankind and despised by the people.
> All who see me mock me;
> > they make mouths at me; they wag their heads;
> "He trusts in the LORD; let him deliver him;
> > let him rescue him, for he delights in him!"
>
> Yet you are he who took me from the womb;
> > you made me trust you at my mother's breasts.

On you was I cast from my birth,
     and from my mother's womb you have been my God.
Be not far from me,
     for trouble is near,
     and there is none to help.

Many bulls encompass me;
     strong bulls of Bashan surround me;
they open wide their mouths at me,
     like a ravening and roaring lion.

I am poured out like water,
     and all my bones are out of joint,
my heart is like wax;
     it is melted within my breast;
my strength is dried up like a potsherd,
     and my tongue sticks to my jaws;
     you lay me in the dust of death.

For dogs encompass me;
     a company of evildoers encircles me;
they have pierced my hands and feet—
I can count all my bones—
     they stare and gloat over me;
they divide my garments among them,
     and for my clothing they cast lots.

But you, O LORD, do not be far off!
     O you my help, come quickly to my aid!
Deliver my soul from the sword,
     my precious life from the power of the dog!
     Save me from the mouth of the lion!
You have rescued me from the horns of the wild oxen!

I will tell of your name to my brothers;
     in the midst of the congregation I will praise you:
You who fear the LORD, praise him!
     All you offspring of Jacob, glorify him,
     and stand in awe of him, all you offspring of Israel!
For he has not despised or abhorred
     the affliction of the afflicted,

and he has not hidden his face from him,
    but has heard, when he cried to him.

From you comes my praise in the great congregation;
    my vows I will perform before those who fear him.
The afflicted shall eat and be satisfied;
    those who seek him shall praise the Lord!
    May your hearts live forever!

All the ends of the earth shall remember
    and turn to the Lord,
and all the families of the nations
    shall worship before you.
For kingship belongs to the Lord,
    and he rules over the nations.

All the prosperous of the earth eat and worship;
    before him shall bow all who go down to the dust,
    even the one who could not keep himself alive.
Posterity shall serve him;
    it shall be told of the Lord to the coming generation;
they shall come and proclaim his righteousness to a people yet
    unborn,
    that he has done it.

LORD'S DAY 17

Q&A 45

Q. *How does Christ's resurrection benefit us?*

A. First, by his resurrection he has overcome death, so that he could make us share in the righteousness which he had obtained for us by his death. Second, by his power we too are raised up to a new life. Third, Christ's resurrection is to us a sure pledge of our glorious resurrection.

We read in Scripture that the Lord Jesus truly and really arose. After his resurrection he had a number of encounters with the disciples and other believers (Acts 1:4; 10:41). Among the first was with doubting Thomas, who was allowed to touch the Lord's body with his own hands (John 20:27). Many saw Jesus, spoke with him, ate with him, and so on (1 Cor. 15:1–8). He remained on earth for forty days after his resurrection.

On the great day of Pentecost Peter told the Jews that in Jesus's resurrection Psalm 16:8–11 (written by David) was fulfilled (Acts 2:25–28). Christ was really buried in a grave but did not decay to dust there. He was taken to heaven, whereas David did not go to heaven but was buried in his grave nearby (Acts 2:29).

The forty days served to confirm the gospel of the resurrection. Occasionally Scripture is silent about those days and speaks as though Christ was received as king in heaven immediately after his resurrection (Eph. 2:6; Rev. 12:5).

In any case, God fully approved the mediatorial work of his

beloved Son. He acknowledged that Christ had completely paid for the forgiveness of our sins (justification). The righteousness that Christ obtained was declared by means of his resurrection to be completely adequate.

More than this, in the second place, by his Spirit equipping for that gospel of his death and resurrection to be proclaimed, Christ brought about great changes in this world. This is how, for example, the Ephesians were rescued from their sinful life as they could still encounter such living around them among their former pagan acquaintances: "But that is not the way you learned Christ!" (Eph. 4:20). The preaching of the truth enjoyed the same blessed results among the Colossians (Col. 1:5–6). The same had happened among the Christians to whom Peter wrote (1 Pet. 1:3). That is why the gospel of the resurrection has been sent to us as well, in order that "we too might walk in newness of life" (Rom. 6:3–4).

Thirdly, everyone who believes in the gospel of Jesus's resurrection will one day also be raised. Jesus promised: "For this is the will of my Father, that everyone who looks on the Son and believes in him should have eternal life, and I will raise him up on the last day" (John 6:40). The apostle Paul communicated the promise that all believers will be raised in glory by using a beautiful figure of speech (1 Cor. 15:20–23). He called the risen Christ "the firstfruits of those who have fallen asleep" (thus, not the first one who was raised). The word *firstfruits* recalls the institution in Israel of giving to God at the feasts of Passover and Pentecost the first gifts and the first loaves of the new harvest. By doing this, Israel acknowledged God's right to the entire harvest. In the resurrection of Christ as well, the entire harvest of believers is included. By his obedience Christ obtained not only the right to rise from the grave himself, but also the right to raise from the grave all those who believe in him (see Acts 26:23; Col. 1:18; Eph. 2:6).

Scripture Reference

Philippians 3:1–21

Finally, my brothers, rejoice in the Lord.

To write the same things to you is no trouble to me and is safe for you. Look out for the dogs, look out for the evildoers, look out for those who mutilate the flesh. For we are the circumcision, who worship by the Spirit of God and glory in Christ Jesus and put no confidence in the flesh—though I myself have reason for confidence in the flesh also. If anyone else thinks he has reason for confidence in the flesh, I have more: circumcised on the eighth day, of the people of Israel, of the tribe of Benjamin, a Hebrew of Hebrews; as to the law, a Pharisee; as to zeal, a persecutor of the church; as to righteousness under the law, blameless. But whatever gain I had, I counted as loss for the sake of Christ. Indeed, I count everything as loss because of the surpassing worth of knowing Christ Jesus my Lord. For his sake I have suffered the loss of all things and count them as rubbish, in order that I may gain Christ and be found in him, not having a righteousness of my own that comes from the law, but that which comes through faith in Christ, the righteousness from God that depends on faith—that I may know him and the power of his resurrection, and may share his sufferings, becoming like him in his death, that by any means possible I may attain the resurrection from the dead.

Not that I have already obtained this or am already perfect, but I press on to make it my own, because Christ Jesus has made me his own. Brothers, I do not consider that I have made it my own. But one thing I do: forgetting what lies behind and straining forward to what lies ahead, I press on toward the goal for the prize of the upward call of God in Christ Jesus. Let those of us who are mature think this way, and if in anything you think otherwise, God will reveal that also to you. Only let us hold true to what we have attained.

Brothers, join in imitating me, and keep your eyes on those who walk according to the example you have in us. For many, of whom I have often told you and now tell you even with tears, walk as enemies of the cross of Christ. Their end is destruction, their god is their belly, and they glory in their shame, with minds set on earthly things. But our citizenship is in heaven, and from it we await a Savior, the Lord Jesus Christ, who will transform our lowly body to be like his glorious body, by the power that enables him even to subject all things to himself.

LORD'S DAY 18

Q&A 46

Q. *What do you confess when you say, he ascended into heaven?*

A. That Christ, before the eyes of his disciples, was taken up from the earth into heaven, and that he is there for our benefit until he comes again to judge the living and the dead.

When our Savior appeared to Mary Magdalene on the morning of his resurrection, she apparently thought that the Lord Jesus would remain with his disciples in the future just like formerly. But he said to her, "Do not cling to me, for I have not yet ascended to the Father; but go to my brothers and say to them, 'I am ascending to my Father and your Father, to my God and your God'" (John 20:17). Forty days later that really happened. On the way to the Mount of Olives, he spoke for the last time about the outpouring of the Holy Spirit that would occur "not many days from now." Then he was taken up before their eyes, and ten days after his ascension the Holy Spirit was poured out.

It was understandable that the disciples continued looking up after he had ascended. At that point, however, two men in white garments suddenly came to stand alongside them, and said: "Men of Galilee, why do you stand looking into heaven? This Jesus, who was taken up from you into heaven, will come in the same way as you saw him go into heaven" (see Acts 1:9–11).

Stephen was permitted to see Jesus there. As the leaders of the

Jewish council were stoning him, Stephen cried out, "Behold, I see the heavens opened, and the Son of Man standing at the right hand of God" (Acts 7:56).

In addition to stating that our Savior *went up* to heaven, the Bible also says that he was *taken* to heaven. That expression means that Christ received the ascension from God as a great reward for all his obedience (Phil. 2:9; Eph. 1:20–23).

The next two questions and answers (47 and 48) unfortunately interrupt the preceding confession. They were based on a remnant of the Roman Catholic doctrine that survived among the Lutherans, namely, involving the bread of the Lord's Supper and the changed body of Christ.

Q&A 47

Q. *Is Christ, then, not with us until the end of the world, as he has promised us?*

A. Christ is true man and true God. With respect to his human nature he is no longer on earth, but with respect to his divinity, majesty, grace, and Spirit he is never absent from us.

Q&A 48

Q. *But are the two natures in Christ not separated from each other if his human nature is not present wherever his divinity is?*

A. Not at all, for his divinity has no limits and is present everywhere. So it must follow that his divinity is indeed beyond the human nature which he has taken on and nevertheless is within this human nature and remains personally united with it.

Christ did indeed promise his disciples that he would be with them until the end of the world. On the other hand, he foretold many times that he would be going away (John 14:2; 16:28; 17:11). But Christ was and is both God and man. Therefore, as God he remains omnipresent and he could promise, "I am with you al-

ways, to the end of the age" (Matt. 28:20). That became evident
on the day of Pentecost, with the outpouring of the Holy Spirit.
But through his resurrection, Christ's body remained a genuinely
human body (Luke 24:39).

Q&A 49

Q. *How does Christ's ascension into heaven benefit us?*

A. First, he is our Advocate in heaven before his Father. Second, we have our flesh in heaven as a sure pledge that he,
our Head, will also take us, his members, up to himself.
Third, he sends us his Spirit as a counterpledge, by whose
power we seek the things that are above, where Christ is,
seated at the right hand of God, and not the things that are
on earth.

The apostle John spoke this way about Christ as our Advocate
in heaven: "My little children, I am writing these things to you
so that you may not sin. But if anyone does sin, we have an advocate with the Father, Jesus Christ the righteous" (1 John 2:1).
Paul writes that "Christ Jesus is the one who died—more than
that, who was raised—who is at the right hand of God, who indeed is interceding for us. Who shall separate us from the love of
Christ?" (see Rom. 8:34–35). Hebrews 9:24 teaches that Christ
went through the heavens to appear before the face of God for
us. This High Priest lives in order to pray for us (Heb. 7:25).

Otherwise it would have been incredible that there should
be people like you and me in heaven! But a real man—Jesus,
the living Jesus who had promised his disciples already before
he died that he would prepare a place for them in his Father's
house (John 14:3)—is there already. That promise is such a genuine guarantee that Paul writes that we are already in heaven,
namely, with our Head. He is the Head of the entire church. So
then, are wherever their head is (Eph. 1:22–23).

The apostle Paul calls Christ not the first, but the firstfruits
of the resurrection (1 Cor. 15:23). The Holy Spirit has spread this
gospel everywhere, and thus many have received faith together

with its fruits. Those fruits are the guarantee of still more to come in the future, as part of the complete inheritance (2 Cor. 1:22; 5:5; Eph. 1:14).

Scripture Reference

Colossians 3:1
If then you have been raised with Christ, seek the things that are above, where Christ is, seated at the right hand of God.

LORD'S DAY 19

Q&A 50

Q. *Why is it added, and sits at the right hand of God?*

A. Christ ascended into heaven to manifest himself there as Head of his church, through whom the Father governs all things.

The right hand is the place of honor. King Solomon, for example, offered his mother a seat on his right (1 Kings 2:19). In the ancient Near East, thrones had more than one seat and were constructed as a sort of platform with room for several people to sit.

In the presence of Caiaphas Jesus foretold that he would soon be sitting at the right hand of Power (Matt. 26:64). And this is what happened. The Lord Jesus was taken into heaven and is now seated at God's right hand (Mark 16:19). Scripture says that Christ has seated himself at the right hand of the throne of the Majesty in heaven (Heb. 1:3; 8:1): Christ the servant, but also completely God.

We should think of this great example when hearing Christ's promise: "The one who conquers, I will grant him to sit with me on my throne, as I also conquered and sat down with my Father on his throne" (Rev. 3:21). For he is our Head and we are members of his body (Col. 1:18; Eph. 1:19–23).

Q&A 51

Q. *How does the glory of Christ, our Head, benefit us?*

A. First, by his Holy Spirit he pours out heavenly gifts upon us, his members. Second, by his power he defends and preserves us against all enemies.

When the outpouring of the Holy Spirit occurred on the great day of Pentecost, the sound of a powerful wind was heard (Acts 2:2). For Greeks and Jews, that was a significant symbol, for Hebrew and Greek each have a word that means both "wind" and "spirit." We also speak of a particular "spirit" that dominates in some circles as a result of conversations, books, magazines, and the like. Just as all the branches and leaves of a tree are blown by the same wind in the same direction, the spirits of all people are also directed in one or another direction either by Satan and his spirits or by God the Holy Spirit.

More than one prophecy was fulfilled with the outpouring of the Holy Spirit. For example, Isaiah 11:2 says of the Child born to David's royal house,

> And the Spirit of the LORD shall rest upon him,
>> the Spirit of wisdom and understanding,
>> the Spirit of counsel and might,
>> the Spirit of knowledge and the fear of the LORD.

(In connection with Q&A 31 we saw how our Savior was baptized and equipped for his work by the Holy Spirit.) And shortly before his departure to heaven, Jesus promised that he would send the Spirit down upon his disciples (John 14:26; 15:26; 16:7; Acts 1:4–5). When the outpouring had occurred, the apostle Peter also pointed to the fulfillment of those promises in what people were now seeing and hearing (Acts 2:32–33).

Moreover, already in the Old Testament dispensation God bestowed gifts of the Spirit. Such gifts could have been given by way of down payment for the enormous mediatorial work of Christ that would follow. For there is salvation in none other (Acts 4:12).

The New Testament dispensation is richer than that of the Old Testament. This is comparable to water that comes first in droplets but then in a torrent. That illustrates the relationship between the Old and New Testaments.

In our day we have the complete Bible! By means of preaching from the Bible, God's Spirit makes people different. He bestows forgiveness of sins and renewal of conduct and life.

As the second fruit of Christ's glory in heaven, the Catechism mentions that Christ "by his power . . . defends and preserves us against all enemies."

Earlier we saw (in Q&A 31, for example, dealing with Christ's kingship) that Christ does not extend his kingdom with the overwhelming force of fire and steel, as the powerbrokers of this world would. On the contrary, there is a great difference between the first century of the Christian church and later times. In the early period Christ helped his church advance in special ways (Mark 16:17–18; Acts 28:5–6; Rom. 15:19; 1 Cor. 1:6; Heb. 2:4). We also read that Stephen, the first martyr who died on Christ's behalf, saw our Savior standing at God's right hand, as if to put an end to that martyring. But it was not yet the Father's time, and so Stephen died (Acts 7:59), under the direction of Saul (Acts 7:58). But this same Saul was converted by Christ in a miraculous manner (Acts 9). These early years enjoyed something quite distinct.

Later, when Paul himself encountered a life-threatening danger, God directed everything in such a way that Paul's nephew discovered the scheme and warned the military person in charge (Acts 23:16). Such miracles, like miracles of healing, occurred more often. But the church of the first century did not yet possess the complete Bible. We do. And that is how the Holy Spirit supplies us wisdom and prepares us for everything that must occur according to the counsel of our heavenly Father (Rev. 1:3; 2:29).

Q&A 52

Q. *What comfort is it to you that Christ will come to judge the living and the dead?*

A. In all my sorrow and persecution I lift up my head and eagerly await as judge from heaven the very same person who before has submitted himself to the judgment of God for my sake, and has removed all the curse from me. He will cast all his and my enemies into everlasting condemnation, but he will take me and all his chosen ones to himself into heavenly joy and glory.

The day of Jesus's return will be a beautiful day for him and for all those who have believed in him as their Savior (Col. 3:4).

The date of that return is unknown. Only our heavenly Father knows (Mark 13:32; Acts 1:7). Wars and rumors of wars will precede it (Mark 13:7–8). Humanity will gradually become more godless, just as in the days before the flood (Matt. 24:37–39). Paul spoke about the man of lawlessness (2 Thess. 2). The apostle John spoke similarly about people who oppose the Christian faith with their so-called piety. For that reason he called them *anti*christs (those *against* Christ; 1 John 2:22; 4:3). Indeed today there are such arrogant people, as was also the case earlier (for example, popes). That is reason enough for us to remain alert (Matt. 25:13).

The Lord Jesus will return in great glory. For this, Scripture uses the Greek word *parousia*. In the time of the apostles this word was used to describe a visit by a prominent person and was applied by the apostles to Christ's return (1 Thess. 2:19; 3:13; 2 Thess. 2:1; Jas. 5:7–8; 2 Pet. 1:16).

On that great day the Lord Jesus will be able to be seen by everyone in the world, just as lightning during a thunderstorm can be seen by everyone (Matt. 24:27). For Christ will come "in the glory of his Father" (Matt. 16:27). There will be signs involving the sun, moon, and stars, and on earth nations will be distraught with fear because of the tumult of the sea and widespread burning, while people will collapse in fear and distress at the things overtaking the world. For the powers of the heavens will be shaken. Then they will see the Son of Man coming in the clouds, with great authority and glory (Luke 21:25–27).

Then the Lord Jesus will awaken all the dead with a voice sounding like a trumpet (John 5:28; 1 Thess. 4:16), and will appear as the Judge of the world. The Father will judge no one, but has given authority to the Lord Jesus, the Man from Nazareth, to execute judgment, because he is the Son of Man (John 5:22, 27; Acts 17:31).

When he executes that judgment, the Lord Jesus will not need to search for the truth. He is God. In a vision John saw that all the dead stood before God and the books were opened and from them the dead were judged (Rev. 20:12).

Nevertheless, we do not need to fear that day if during our life we have believed in the Lord Jesus as our Savior (John 3:18). He will awaken us, and we will be taken to meet him in the air (1 Thess. 4:17). He will welcome us as the blessed of his Father (Matt. 25:34), but to the wicked he will say, "Depart from me, you cursed, into the eternal fire prepared for the devil and his angels" (Matt. 25:41).

Scripture References

Psalm 110:1–7

The LORD says to my Lord:
    "Sit at my right hand,
until I make your enemies your footstool."

The LORD sends forth from Zion
    your mighty scepter.
    Rule in the midst of your enemies!
Your people will offer themselves freely
    on the day of your power,
    in holy garments;
from the womb of the morning,
    the dew of your youth will be yours.
The LORD has sworn
    and will not change his mind,

"You are a priest forever
  after the order of Melchizedek."

The Lord is at your right hand;
  he will shatter kings on the day of his wrath.
He will execute judgment among the nations,
  filling them with corpses;
he will shatter chiefs
  over the wide earth.
He will drink from the brook by the way;
  therefore he will lift up his head."

Matthew 28:18–20
And Jesus came and said to them, "All authority in heaven and on earth has been given to me. Go therefore and make disciples of all nations, baptizing them in the name of the Father and of the Son and of the Holy Spirit, teaching them to observe all that I have commanded you. And behold, I am with you always, to the end of the age."

Titus 2:13
Waiting for our blessed hope, the appearing of the glory of our great God and Savior Jesus Christ.

1 Peter 4:13
But rejoice insofar as you share Christ's sufferings, that you may also rejoice and be glad when his glory is revealed.

LORD'S DAY 20

Q&A 53

Q. *What do you believe concerning the Holy Spirit?*

A. First, he is, together with the Father and the Son, true and eternal God. Second, he is also given to me, to make me by true faith share in Christ and all his benefits, to comfort me, and to remain with me forever.

As the Lord Jesus was preparing to go from earth back to heaven, he gave his disciples significant instruction from Scripture, the greatest part of which had already been written down (the Old Testament), along with the command to proclaim the gospel everywhere, among all the nations, baptizing them in the name of the Father, the Son, and the Holy Spirit (Matt. 28:19). From this it is evident that the Holy Spirit is God just as much as the Father and the Son are God.

The origin of the Bible is to be credited especially to the Holy Spirit. He inspired prophets and writers. It was a work that took centuries.

Along with the Father and the Son, the Holy Spirit participated in the great work of creation (Gen. 1:2; Job 26:13; Ps. 33:6). He also equipped Bezalel and Oholiab to construct the tabernacle (Exod. 31:1–11), supplied Samson with the courage and strength to fight against the Philistines (Judg. 14:6, 19), equipped John the Baptist to serve as Jesus's forerunner (Luke 1:15, 80), and fulfilled the prophecy of Isaiah 11:2 regarding Christ:

And the Spirit of the LORD shall rest upon him,
   the Spirit of wisdom and understanding,
   the Spirit of counsel and might,
   the Spirit of knowledge and the fear of the LORD.

Our Savior was conceived by his mother through the Holy Spirit, baptized by the Holy Spirit, and led by the Spirit to the contest with Satan in the wilderness. Through God's Spirit, an innocent Jesus sacrificed himself to God (Heb. 9:14), after which he was also exalted by the Holy Spirit (Rom. 1:4; 8:11; 1 Tim. 3:16; 1 Pet. 3:18–19). When he had sat down at the Father's right hand, the Father granted the Spirit to him in such abundance that he could pour out the Spirit upon his apostles (Acts 2:17, 33). Scripture speaks of him as the Spirit of Jesus (Acts 16:7), the Spirit of Christ (Rom. 8:9), or the Spirit of Jesus Christ (Phil. 1:19). The apostles were equipped for their work by the Holy Spirit as the promised *Parakletos* ("Paraclete"), which means Advocate, Helper, Intercessor, Teacher, Comforter, and Counselor (John 14:16, 26; see also Acts and the Epistles).

For the writer of the Epistle to the Hebrews, the claim that Scripture originated from God the Holy Spirit is so obvious that he frequently cites Scripture with the introductory words "as the Holy Spirit says" (3:7; see also 9:8; 10:15). The apostle Paul wrote that all Scripture was given by God (2 Tim. 3:16). There he used the word *theopneustos*, a word many will immediately recognize as containing the words *theos* (God) and *pneuma* (Spirit).

So Scripture is the voice of God the Holy Spirit. Therefore, according to their conscience the scribes in Jesus's day actually should have agreed with him, but instead they kept on opposing him, going as far as ascribing his miracles to his cooperation with Satan (Matt. 12:24). What terrible blasphemy this was, and Jesus warned very sternly about it as being the unforgiveable sin (Matt. 12:31). Stephen sounded the same warning to the members of the Jewish council. They were acting just like Israel had formerly when some people resisted the Holy Spirit (Acts 7:51). The writer of the Letter to the Hebrews also warned against that sin (Heb. 2:2–4; 6:4). Did his readers perhaps wish to crucify the Son of God for a second time (Heb. 10:29)? Whoever rejects

God's Word and thereby opposes the Holy Spirit is lost without any possibility of rescue!

Occasionally the Holy Spirit is called the Spirit of sanctification, because this is his special work.

He began this work already with those ancestors who were still pagans. From Antioch he sent out Barnabas and Saul to preach the gospel, not only to Jews but also to Gentiles, for example, teaching the Galatians (the term *Galatian* is a combination of *Gauls* and *Celts*, Germanic pagans by descent) to address God as their Father (Gal. 1:3–5; 4:6; the Hebrew word for "father" was *'abba*). Following their preaching in Asia Minor, the Holy Spirit led the apostles westward, starting in the region of Macedonia (Acts 16:6). After that, the gospel continued westward throughout Europe. At that point many others also were included in the fellowship of God's covenant, sharing in Christ and his saving work. We must be obedient to that covenant. For then the Spirit's sanctification advances in our hearts and lives. And thus these words apply to us as well: "Since we have these promises, beloved, let us cleanse ourselves from every defilement of body and spirit, bringing holiness to completion in the fear of God" (2 Cor. 7:1).

God gave our Christian ancestors the same covenant he gave long ago to Abraham (Gen. 17:7; Gal. 3:8; 1 Pet. 2:10), and so we also were born as "holy"— separated from the world and appointed to the service of God. For that reason we were also baptized. Christian parents must make sure they tell and clearly explain this to their children. For then they are being obedient instruments of the Holy Spirit. In this way the preaching of the gospel must begin in our lives already during our Christian youth. In this way we must learn early to believe in Christ. That faith will make us new people and liberate us from the slavery of sin. Occasionally Scripture speaks very concisely. It does not always declare expansively that God's Word works faith and that this faith regenerates us, but it does say at times very concisely that God's Word regenerates us (Jas. 1:18; 1 Pet. 1:23). At other times Scripture says very concisely that God's Spirit works faith within our hearts (1 Cor. 12:13).

Scripture References

Mark 12:9
"What will the owner of the vineyard do? He will come and destroy the tenants and give the vineyard to others."

Luke 3:16
John answered them all, saying, "I baptize you with water, but he who is mightier than I is coming, the strap of whose sandals I am not worthy to untie. He will baptize you with the Holy Spirit and fire."

Acts 2:1–13
When the day of Pentecost arrived, they were all together in one place. And suddenly there came from heaven a sound like a mighty rushing wind, and it filled the entire house where they were sitting. And divided tongues as of fire appeared to them and rested on each one of them. And they were all filled with the Holy Spirit and began to speak in other tongues as the Spirit gave them utterance.

Now there were dwelling in Jerusalem Jews, devout men from every nation under heaven. And at this sound the multitude came together, and they were bewildered, because each one was hearing them speak in his own language. And they were amazed and astonished, saying, "Are not all these who are speaking Galileans? And how is it that we hear, each of us in his own native language? Parthians and Medes and Elamites and residents of Mesopotamia, Judea and Cappadocia, Pontus and Asia, Phrygia and Pamphylia, Egypt and the parts of Libya belonging to Cyrene, and visitors from Rome, both Jews and proselytes, Cretans and Arabians—we hear them telling in our own tongues the mighty works of God." And all were amazed and perplexed, saying to one another, "What does this mean?" But others mocking said, "They are filled with new wine."

Romans 11:17
But if some of the branches were broken off, and you, although a wild olive shoot, were grafted in among the others and now share in the nourishing root of the olive tree.

LORD'S DAY 21

Q&A 54

Q. *What do you believe concerning the holy catholic Christian church?*

A. I believe that the Son of God, out of the whole human race, from the beginning of the world to its end, gathers, defends, and preserves for himself, by his Spirit and Word, in the unity of the true faith, a church chosen to everlasting life. And I believe that I am and forever shall remain a living member of it.

In understanding the language of the Creed, it makes a big difference whether we use the single word *believe* or speak of *believing in*.

We can use the single word *believe* with respect to people—to believe someone or not to believe them. But the Creed uses the phrase *believe in* only with respect to God, as when the Apostles' Creed begins with "I believe in God." But when it comes to confessing about the church, we say, "I believe a holy catholic Christian church." Why do we make of that difference? Because the church is not divine. No matter how highly we esteem the church, the church consists of people.

This does not mean, however, that we may claim anything about the church that we want. We must be instructed about the church only from Holy Scripture.

As far as the meaning of the term *church* is concerned, that term unfortunately does not come all that directly from the Bible, but more from the French word *église*. It was imported directly into the Gallic language from the Greek word *ekklēsia*. Our term *church* contains the term *kyrios* ("Master"), referring to Christ. It is unfortunate that the term *church* is also used to refer to a wooden or stone building. Our English term *congregation* indicates that a group of people is in view, those who live together in the fellowship or communion of faith in Christ.

By the term *church* Scripture occasionally means simply the local church, situated somewhere in a city or town. Paul wrote a letter to the *ekklēsiai* (the plural of *ekklēsia*) in Galatia. But when the Lord Jesus promised that he would build his church on the confession of Peter, and that the powers of the realm of the dead would not prevail against her, the Savior was obviously speaking about the church in its larger sense (Matt. 16:18).

We confess concerning the church that she is a church chosen unto eternal life. We may learn what this means, for example, from the introduction to the Letter to the Ephesians. How joyful Paul was when he saw that God was implementing his plan to make believers out of people from the Gentile world more often than previously. Formerly, when many Gentiles wanted to join God's people, they had to satisfy many requirements. The males needed to be circumcised, and the food and clothing were entirely different. But that "dividing wall of hostility" (Eph. 2:14) was removed through Christ's death and suffering. God could now fulfill his ancient plan to grant mercy also to the Gentiles on a far wider scale than ever.

From this we learn that we may talk joyfully and thankfully about election. Apart from election we would still be pagans. Jesus himself was comforted by election when he experienced severe opposition. He said, "All that the Father gives me will come to me" (John 6:37; see also Rom. 8:28–30 and Acts 13:48). Lift your eyes to the starry sky in particular. God is so wonderfully powerful! How foolish that we sometimes hesitate to believe everything that the Bible tells us about him!

Sometimes the church is called a temple (Acts 4:1; Eph. 2:20–21), or a body whose head is Christ (Eph. 1:23), or a bride (John 3:29; 2 Cor. 11:2; Rev. 22:17).

That church has expanded today throughout the entire world. The Jewish people have lost their special privilege. To become a member of the church, a Gentile no longer needs to undergo any circumcision of his body (Gal 3:23–26). This change generated severe opposition among the so-called Judaizers (see our discussion of Q&A 30), but Paul wrote that there is neither Jew nor Greek, slave nor free, male nor female, but we are all one in Christ Jesus (Gal 3:28).

When the Catechism says that this church is not only gathered by God's Son, but also defended and preserved, we must not suppose that according to the Catechism Christians are never called to suffer. On the contrary, Stephen was stoned, and how many have followed him! But God's church will never be destroyed. That reality was shown already with the flood, when Noah was saved in the ark. In the dangerous time of King Ahab, it was not only Elijah who survived, but there were also seven thousand who had not bowed the knee to Baal. God's people were led away into captivity, but a remnant returned to Palestine and from that remnant our Savior was born.

There is every reason to call the church *Christian*, since Christ is the Head of the church, and the bride takes the name of her Bridegroom.

The church is also called *catholic* or *universal*. Originally people did not need to use that word. Later, however, Christians came with unbiblical teachings and became disobedient to the teaching of Christ and the apostles. At that point the need arose among the faithful to call their church *catholic*, a word that comes from the Greek word meaning "universal." With that term people wanted to declare that the church believes only what has been read in God's Word, the Scriptures. Paul wrote, "If anyone teaches a different doctrine and does not agree with the sound words of our Lord Jesus Christ and the teaching that accords with godliness, he is puffed up with conceit and understands nothing" (1 Tim. 6:3–4a; see 2 Tim. 1:13). Whoever either takes away from or adds to the teaching of Scripture forsakes the catholic church. The unity of the faithful members of the church does not consist in the fact that they gather together in one place. Today that is not possible, due to the language barrier, among other reasons.

The unity of church members together consists in their unity with the Word of God, the Bible. Only Christians who are bound together in this way can legitimately claim the title *catholic*. (The Greek-based word *ecumenical* originally meant the same thing.)

By confessing that "I am and forever shall remain a living member" of this church, we hear the Catechism distinguishing between living and dead members. Jesus said, "Not everyone who says to me, 'Lord, Lord,' will enter the kingdom of heaven, but the one who does the will of my Father who is in heaven" (Matt. 7:21). He also said, "Every branch in me that does not bear fruit he [the Father] takes away" (John 15:2). For that reason the faithful church is sometimes obligated to cut off "dead" members from her body by means of excommunication (see Lord's Day 31).

Finally, believers confess here not only that they are living members of the church today, but also that they forever shall remain living members of the church. In Lord's Day 20, Question and Answer 53, we have already confessed that the Holy Spirit was not only given to us but also will abide with us. This is repeated here and discussed more extensively in the last chapter of the Canons of Dort, which bears the title "The perseverance of the saints." With this formulation we are not confessing that we can never sin again. Scripture teaches us differently—think of David and Peter (Rom. 7:15–25; 1 John 3:9). But there is forgiveness (1 John 2:1).

Q&A 55

Q. *What do you understand by the communion of saints?*

A. First, that believers, all and everyone, as members of Christ have communion with him and share in all his treasures and gifts. Second, that everyone is duty-bound to use his gifts readily and cheerfully for the benefit and well-being of the other members.

The Catechism explains the article concerning the communion of the saints by returning first to our communion with the Lord

Jesus, and only then discussing the communion of believers with each other.

Our communion with Christ will be fully manifested only when Christ returns to earth one day: "When Christ who is your life appears, then you also will appear with him in glory" (Col. 3:4; see also Rom. 8:17; 1 John 3:2; Phil. 3:21). He will acknowledge us before his Father (Matt. 10:32). Then we will live in paradise in full communion with Christ.

But that is not our situation at the moment. Christ is still in heaven, "hidden with Christ in God" (Col. 3:3). Nevertheless, from heaven he has done quite a bit for his people. He sent his Spirit; he provided for the Scriptures to be completed; through the apostolic preaching he brought us into the covenant of grace together with Abraham, Isaiah, Stephen, and all the saints who are already asleep. So there is communion between Christ and his entire church, and as a result, among all believers together. This communion is demonstrated by believers loving one another and caring for each other, just like brothers and sisters in a family, and just like the members of a body (e.g., as the hand cares for the arms and legs, as the eye cares for the hand, etc.). This is gloriously described in Acts 2. The Christians in Jerusalem persevered in the teaching of the apostles (stories about the Lord Jesus) and in fellowship, in the breaking of bread and in prayers. They cared for each other. No one suffered any lack. They praised God together in prayers and in songs. At a later time Christians there were persecuted, but they received "house or brothers or sisters or mother or father or children or lands" (Mark 10:29).

In every place Christians have the right to enlist the most suited among them to serve in the name of Jesus in the offices of teacher, elder, and deacon. In regulated gatherings Scripture is explained, and baptism and the Lord's Supper are administered, usually on Sunday. Every believer collaborates with regular visiting, encouraging, and helping.

Q&A 56

Q. *What do you believe concerning the forgiveness of sins?*

A. I believe that God, because of Christ's satisfaction, will no more remember my sins, nor my sinful nature, against which I have to struggle all my life, but will graciously grant me the righteousness of Christ, that I may never come into condemnation.

It is universally known how the glorious light of the gospel of the forgiveness of sins was almost extinguished in the medieval church, and how deep the darkness was that surrounded Christianity. The Bible virtually became a closed book. People no longer knew Christ as the Savior sent by the Father in mercy to save sinners, but rather as the future judge of the whole world, who would cast not only all pagans into perdition but also Christians who had a shortage of good works. That was why Luther discontinued studying with the Faculty of the Arts in Erfurt and became a monk, in order to become perfect. He became sick as a result. An elderly monastic brother consoled him with the Apostles' Creed, which contains the words "I believe ... the forgiveness of sins."

Immediately after the first sin of our first parents, our heavenly Father promised to send a Savior. Of course God is righteous, but he treated Moses like a friend (Exod. 33:11). He made himself known to Moses as "The LORD, the LORD, a God merciful and gracious, slow to anger, and abounding in steadfast love and faithfulness, keeping steadfast love for thousands, forgiving iniquity and transgression and sin, but who will by no means clear the guilty, visiting the iniquity of the fathers on the children and the children's children, to the third and the fourth generation" (Exod. 34:6–7). The church of the old dispensation confessed,

> O LORD our God, you answered them;
>   you were a forgiving God to them,
>   but an avenger of their wrongdoings (Ps. 99:8).

Read especially Daniel 9:4–5, 19: "O Lord, the great and awesome God, who keeps covenant and steadfast love with those who love him and keep his commandments, we have sinned and done wrong and acted wickedly and rebelled, turning aside from your commandments and rules. . . . O Lord, hear; O Lord, forgive. . . ." Read Psalm 103:12: "As far as the east is from the west, so far does he remove our transgressions from us." Already in the Old Testament God forgave many people their sins, including David, so that he composed Psalm 32, which begins this way: "Blessed is the one whose transgression is forgiven, whose sin is covered." But the full light of God's compassion shone when he honored his covenant with the patriarchs and sent his Son to atone for the sins of the whole world (Titus 2:11; 3:4–7). First God gave his Son and made peace with the world on the basis of Christ's satisfaction (2 Cor. 5:18–19).

How tragic, then, that the Christian church lost this treasure through neglect. How fortunate that in the period of the great reformation of the church the light dawned once again. As Christ said once, "Truly, truly, I say to you, whoever hears my word and believes him who sent me has eternal life. He does not come into judgment, but has passed from death to life" (John 5:24). He himself taught us to pray the Lord's Prayer, where we find not only the petition "Give us this day our daily bread" but also this one: "And forgive us our debts." We will have to pray that prayer each day.

Scripture References

Psalm 130:3-4
> If you, O Lord, should mark iniquities,
>   O Lord, who could stand?
> But with you there is forgiveness,
>   that you may be feared.

Psalm 133:1
> Behold, how good and pleasant it is
>   when brothers dwell in unity!

Mark 10:29-30
Jesus said, "Truly, I say to you, there is no one who has left house or brothers or sisters or mother or father or children or lands, for my sake and for the gospel, who will not receive a hundredfold now in this time, houses and brothers and sisters and mothers and children and lands, with persecutions, and in the age to come eternal life."

Ephesians 4:1-7
I therefore, a prisoner for the Lord, urge you to walk in a manner worthy of the calling to which you have been called, with all humility and gentleness, with patience, bearing with one another in love, eager to maintain the unity of the Spirit in the bond of peace. There is one body and one Spirit—just as you were called to the one hope that belongs to your call—one Lord, one faith, one baptism, one God and Father of all, who is over all and through all and in all. But grace was given to each one of us according to the measure of Christ's gift.

1 John 1:9
If we confess our sins, he is faithful and just to forgive us our sins and to cleanse us from all unrighteousness.

LORD'S DAY 22

Q&A 57

Q. *What comfort does the resurrection of the body offer you?*

A. Not only shall my soul after this life immediately be taken up to Christ, my Head, but also this my flesh, raised by the power of Christ, shall be reunited with my soul and made like Christ's glorious body.

Q&A 58

Q. *What comfort do you receive from the article about the life everlasting?*

A. Since I now already feel in my heart the beginning of eternal joy, I shall after this life possess perfect blessedness, such as no eye has seen, nor ear heard, nor the heart of man conceived—a blessedness in which to praise God forever.

Today we would say some things in Lord's Day 22 differently than people did when it was composed. But the Catechism correctly asks what *comfort* the last two articles of the Apostles' Creed offer. We experience that, for example, when on a certain day in the week we have lost a beloved member of our family or relatives through death. On the next Sunday we hear the whole congregation confess its faith in the gospel of the resurrection and of eternal life. That can fill us with emotion. This is something that no one needs to feel ashamed of. The Lord Jesus also wept at the grave of Lazarus (John 11:35) and sympathized with the widow who must have missed her son, the young man from Nain (Luke 7:13). Already during his humiliation, Jesus performed these miracles, thereby returning temporal life to these people who had died. He had humbled himself deeply, since during his humiliation he possessed the power to raise the dead (John 10:18). He used this power only sparingly. But when he returns one day on the clouds of heaven, he will permanently raise all those who loved him, not to live temporarily but to live eternally, without ever again being frightened by that terrible death.

Unfortunately, after the departure of the apostles, a doctrine entered the Christian church that is completely unknown to Holy Scripture, namely, the doctrine of purgatory. It was officially adopted for the first time under Pope Gregory the Great (540–604). Since 998, the feast of All Saints has been celebrated on November 1. But fortunately Luther and other church reformers wanted nothing to do with this error. In Scripture we never find the word *purgatory* or anything close to it, nor do we find anywhere the command to pray for the dead who are supposedly staying in a kind of waiting room before being allowed to enter heaven. Nor do we read a single word about the prayers of the dead on their own behalf. In fact, these fantasies constitute an affront to our Savior, our only Redeemer, whose work as our Surety needs no supplement.

It is entirely mistaken to argue that once a person has been adequately purified in purgatory, he may enter heaven. With the exception of the prophet Elijah, we read only that the Lord Jesus went to heaven. This applies to no one else. We are taught concerning David that he did not ascend to heaven (Acts 2:34), but that he slept and was buried with his fathers (Acts 13:36).

When will the resurrection of the dead occur? When the Lord Jesus returns. Then, with the summons of an archangel and with the sound of God's trumpet, he will descend from heaven, and those who have died in Christ will rise first. After that, those who are living and are left behind will be taken up together with them on the cloud, to meet the Lord in the air, all in the blink of an eye. And thus we will always be with the Lord. Admonish, or better, *encourage*, each other with these words (1 Thess. 4:16–18).

The blood of Jesus, God's Son, cleanses us from all sin (1 John 1:7). When Jesus returns we will receive immortality, also called eternal life.

We must use these words carefully. Since the Holy Spirit works faith in our hearts and has this faith govern all our activities, we speak of having *spiritual life* right now. But Scripture teaches that no human being possesses *immortality* right now. On the contrary, the apostle Paul directs us to God, "who alone has immortality, who dwells in unapproachable light, whom no one has ever seen or can see. To him be honor and eternal dominion. Amen" (1 Tim. 6:16). *Spiritual life* is a present reality, and we receive *eternal life* in the future age (Mark 10:30).

The question is often asked, "But the Lord Jesus himself said that whoever believes in him has eternal life (John 3:36). It is a present possession. That is not future tense but present tense. How do you explain that?"

We answer this question by referring to the promissory speech of God that appears frequently in Scripture. Although our God did not give Abraham the land of Canaan as his ordinary possession, he talked occasionally with Abraham about it as though he had already done so (Gen. 35:12). Later the Israelites heard Moses speak occasionally about the land of Canaan in the same way as they traveled through the wilderness, making reference to "your land." But they were still trekking through the sand.

We too may accept by faith that our loved ones, whom we miss on account of their death, will be raised out of their graves safely by virtue of God's promise. We accept this so certainly that we sometimes speak as though they were already alive again. But that is not yet the case. The apostle wrote, "For this perishable body must put on the imperishable, and this mortal body must put on immortality" (1 Cor. 15:53).

But if you are a believer on your sickbed, you earnestly long for your own death but then comfort yourself with the knowledge that only three things need to happen yet. First, your sickbed will end after a certain number of days; second, you will lie in the grave, but that lasts zero days for you; and then third, our beloved Savior will come with all those who have believed in him having been freed from death and quickened with inexpressible salvation. So on your deathbed you close your eyes, but shortly thereafter you will see Jesus. Eyes closed, eyes open.

Let us then live in the comfort that comes from trusting in the gospel about which the apostle John writes, "And this is the promise that he made to us—eternal life" (1 John 2:25).

Maybe someone is wondering what Jesus meant by what he said to the converted murderer on the cross: "Today you will be with me in Paradise" (Luke 23:43). In John 19:31 we read that the Jewish leaders wanted the corpses of the three men taken care of, and so they allowed them to die. The converted murderer must have died after some time. But for this dead murderer as well, his sojourn in the grave would last zero minutes before paradise opened for him. This means that for him and for all who have loved Jesus, the resurrection will occur in the blink of an eye, in a speck of time, an indivisible moment (1 Cor. 15:52). This may comfort us as well, when we are sick or get old and approach death. We will die at the time appointed by God, it is true, but then we will immediately be raised and go to meet Jesus (1 Thess. 4:13–18; see 1 Cor. 15:50–58).

Our English Bibles use the word *soul* differently than Lord's Day 22 does. For example, from Genesis 2:7 we learn that God formed man from the dust of the ground and blew into his nostrils the breath of life, and in this way man became a living soul (*nephesh*). In Hebrew one can speak of a "dead" soul (Num. 6:6). The word *soul* can refer to someone's desire (Prov. 27:7; Ps. 107:5). The word *soul* occasionally refers to oneself, as in Matthew 16:25: "For whoever would save his life [*soul*, himself] will lose it, but whoever loses his life [*soul*, himself] for my sake will find it." In the parallel passage of Luke 9:25 we read, "What does it profit a man if he gains the whole world and loses or forfeits himself [*his soul*]?" Similarly the meaning of the word *soul* in James 1:21 is best rendered as referring to one's self: "The Word brings about life change. One must think here of the entire life, not only of what people often identify as the soul. The entire person, as he exists, is redeemed by Christ, if he accepts the Word" (*Korte Verklaring*, a classic Dutch biblical commentary). Whoever has lost his life for Jesus's sake (for examples, consider the many Christian martyrs) will find it.

LORD'S DAY 23

Q&A 59

Q. *But what does it help you now that you believe all this?*

A. In Christ I am righteous before God and heir to life everlasting.

In Protestant circles it sometimes is said, inaccurately, that Roman Catholics insist that they are saved through their good works, whereas we insist that we are saved only through the atoning merits of our Lord Jesus Christ. An alert Roman Catholic would probably quickly reply, "That's not true. We believe that the grace that the church bestows is indispensable." Roman Catholics genuinely believe this. According to them, an unbaptized infant who dies goes to hell. They believe that an adult can be saved from so-called mortal sins only through the "grace" that the church supplies through the so-called sacrament of confession. In this connection good works are counted. Thus one is saved through the sum total of the equation: (1) the Christ of the sacrament plus (2) good works.

When our ancestors freed themselves from Roman Catholic teaching, they completely rejected both of these claims. They rejected not only the mistaken doctrine about good works but also the mistaken doctrine about the sacraments, according to which "grace" is automatically infused in a person, as drinking water is poured into a glass. This is wrong! Scripture teaches that we are not justified automatically through baptism, but only through faith.

We believe that when a baby is born to us and is brought to the church to be baptized, it need not first pass by the sacristy in order first to profess faith. Nor do we believe that an unbaptized infant cannot be saved. The infant enters the gathering of the church *as a member with full rights*. This explains the insistence in the liturgical formulary that a baby born to a believing parent ought to be baptized.

It's too bad that Roman Catholics do not believe this. According to them, an unbaptized infant who dies goes to hell. That is why it is necessary to pass through the sacristy. There the child makes confession through the word of the godparents, and only then is the infant baptized. In this way, the one baptized is both regenerated and justified.

But this is all wrong.

Grace is not something that one pours into another. The word *grace* is a synonym for *favor*. This too is not infused anywhere but rather is shown to a person. And regeneration is not a momentary thing. Nor is the confessing of the faith of a child through the words of so-called godparents anything but a fantasy.

Scripture teaches that the children of Christians are baptized as those who possess God's covenant promises just like their parents. Moreover, this is assured to them through baptism. When we are grown, thanks to the instruction of our parents we may confess that we were born both as a child of Adam and also simultaneously as heirs of the covenant who may believingly rejoice in the gospel that the blood of Jesus Christ cleanses us from all our sins.

Q&A 60

Q. *How are you righteous before God?*

A. Only by true faith in Jesus Christ. Although my conscience accuses me that I have grievously sinned against all God's commandments, have never kept any of them, and am still inclined to all evil, yet God, without any merit of my own, out of mere grace, imputes to me the perfect satisfaction, righteousness, and holiness of Christ. He grants these to me as if I had never had nor committed any sin, and as if I myself had accomplished all the obedience that Christ has rendered for me, if only I accept this gift with a believing heart.

There are various words here whose meaning we must understand well. We would observe initially that we can learn to understand a word's meaning if we learn to comprehend its opposite. In Scripture we often find in opposition to the word *righteous* the word *wicked*. Before the destruction of Sodom and Gomorrah, Abraham said to God, "Will you indeed sweep away the righteous with the wicked?" (Gen. 18:23). We are told that the elderly Simeon was "righteous and devout" (Luke 2:25). The word *righteous* is a synonym for living "upright in heart" (Pss. 32:11; 97:11). According to Psalms 37 and 112, "the righteous" take great delight in God's commandments, something that arises not from ourselves but through the Holy Spirit, who places us under the spell of God's Word and inclines our heart to the fear of the Lord. This applies to all people, except the Lord Jesus. He is frequently called simply the Righteous One. A "righteous one" is someone who delights in keeping all of God's commandments, someone who acts obediently.

The word *righteous* is related to the noun *righteousness*. A synonym of this word is *integrity*. The opposite of "righteousness" is "wickedness" (Ps. 45:7). When Job was accused by his friends of leading a wicked past, he rejected those accusations by saying, "I put on righteousness, and it clothed me," and he spoke among other things about his mercy toward widows

and orphans (Job 29:14). The word *righteousness* means a believing obedience to God's law. That word *believing* belongs in
the definition, for the Pharisees thought they had a lot of righteousness because they kept God's commandments with intense
zeal, but Jesus declared, "I tell you, unless your righteousness
exceed that of the scribes and Pharisees, you will never enter
the kingdom of heaven" (Matt. 5:20). The righteousness of the
righteous is their upright obedience to the law of God, to all of
God's commandments.

The verb "to justify" leads us to think, for example, of the
judge in Proverbs 17:15: "He who justifies the wicked and he who
condemns the righteous are both alike an abomination to the
LORD." We think as well of Romans 8:33–34a: "Who shall bring
any charge against God's elect? It is God who justifies. Who is
to condemn?" Instead of using the word *condemn*, our ancestors
used to speak of "damning" and of "damnation." We should understand clearly that "to justify" means "to acquit."

But someone may say that if a judge may not acquit a guilty
person, how then is it possible that God does not condemn a
sinner like David (think of his conduct with Uriah and Bathsheba, 2 Sam. 11)? We see the same with Paul, who persecuted
the church of God. Nevertheless, Paul wrote shortly before
his death that the crown of righteousness had been laid up for
him (2 Tim. 4:8). In short, Scripture teaches that God justifies
the ungodly (Rom. 4:5). It says so in the Bible. We ask how
that's possible.

From Scripture this seems hardly to be a riddle. Even though
the church of the old dispensation was not permitted to know
everything as clearly as we do, they looked at the image of the
cherubim that stood on the mercy seat of the ark, on which the
blood of atonement was to be sprinkled (Exod. 25:20; 1 Pet.
1:17–19). If God justifies sinners not just like David and Paul
but also like us, that is because God wanted to be so gracious
toward us that he gave us his own beloved Son as a Lamb upon
whom he placed all our sins (Isa. 53): "In this the love of God
was made manifest among us, that God sent his only Son into
the world, so that we might live through him" (1 John 4:9). One
day John the Baptist saw Jesus Christ walking in the middle of

a group of people and directed his own disciples to Jesus with the words "Behold the Lamb of God who takes away the sin of the world" (John 1:29). God has granted us Christ as Mediator and Surety. Through the coming and work of Jesus, it is not at all detestable when God acquits such people like us on the basis of Christ's perfect mediatorial work. In Romans 3:25 the apostle calls Christ a propitiation. He uses a Greek word used already by the Greek translation of the Old Testament, the Septuagint, to translate the Hebrew word for an atonement covering. For that reason Paul also calls the death of Christ a demonstration of God's righteousness (Rom. 3:25). What seemed to us initially to be a riddle appears now to be exceedingly fair. For the Lord Jesus has become our righteousness.

But there is still this question: How does that obedience, that righteousness of Christ, become ours?

Let's use this analogy. A man who is dirt poor receives from a wealthy person a bank note that he can repeatedly take to the bank and ask to receive as much as he needs. If the man trusts and follows up on that offer, he can pay off his debts. That's also what happens when a sinner is justified. Throughout his life he receives what he needs just as often as he trusts God's promise in his Word, namely, that God grants forgiveness of sins to everyone who believes that the blood of Jesus Christ cleanses from all sin.

This gospel used to be known only to the Hebrew church, but since Christ's ascension and pouring out of the Holy Spirit (on Pentecost), it must be preached throughout the entire world (Matt. 28:19–20). It may—no, it *must*—be preached everywhere: "Whoever believes in him is not condemned" (John 3:18). In many other places Scripture tells us that forgiveness of sins is received through faith in Christ (Acts 26:18), that one is justified through faith (Rom. 3:28), and that we are justified by faith (Rom. 5:1), and so on.

Q&A 61

Q. *Why do you say that you are righteous only by faith?*

A. Not that I am acceptable to God on account of the worthiness of my faith, for only the satisfaction, righteousness, and holiness of Christ is my righteousness before God. I can receive this righteousness and make it my own by faith only.

"Only." "Only" by faith in Jesus Christ. When our ancestors cast off the yoke of Rome, the Roman Catholics were very offended by that little word *only*. For it wasn't in the Bible. So was it necessary then? And yet, isn't the word *Trinity* absent from the Bible, too? If the Roman Catholics had simply been willing to see what was meant with that little word *only*, how Scriptural it was: it seeks to remove every kind of self-generated supplement to the merits of Christ, and to stay close to Paul's declaration against the Judaizers, that we are justified "for nothing" (*gratis*) (Rom. 3:24). The Latin phrase *sola fide* usually is rendered in English with the phrase "by faith alone."

Scripture References

Romans 3:25–26
Whom God put forward as a propitiation by his blood, to be received by faith. This was to show God's righteousness, because in his divine forbearance he had passed over former sins. It was to show his righteousness at the present time, so that he might be just and the justifier of the one who has faith in Jesus.

Romans 4:5
And to the one who does not work but believes in him who justifies the ungodly, his faith is counted as righteousness.

Romans 5:6
For while we were still weak, at the right time Christ died for the ungodly.

Ephesians 1:5–7
He predestined us for adoption as sons through Jesus Christ, according to the purpose of his will, to the praise of his glorious grace, with which he has blessed us in the Beloved. In him we have redemption through his blood, the forgiveness of our trespasses, according to the riches of his grace.

Lord's Day 24

Q&A 62

Q. *But why can our good works not be our righteousness before God, or at least a part of it?*

A. Because the righteousness which can stand before God's judgment must be absolutely perfect and in complete agreement with the law of God, whereas even our best works in this life are all imperfect and defiled with sin.

Ancient Israel lacked much, compared with us. For Israel did not yet have a complete Bible and could not read in the apostolic writings of the New Testament about the fulfillment of the Old Testament shadows. Even so, God's grace had been wonderfully preached to Israel, when, for example, someone came bringing a burnt offering to the altar: "He shall lay his hand on the head of the burnt offering, and it shall be accepted for him to make atonement for him" (Lev. 1:4).

Didn't that ordinance communicate clearly? It comes from the time of Moses. His additional work, like the book of Deuteronomy, has been praised highly.

Later teachers thought it necessary to add various regulations to God's commandments. Their name is all too familiar to us: they were the Pharisees. John the Baptist summoned these men to repentance from their self-directed religion and directed them to the fulfillment of the shadows of Moses's law by the Lord Jesus, who had come to earth at this point. John

said about Jesus, "Behold, the Lamb of God, who takes away
the sins of the world!" (John 1:29). Later Jesus himself warned
his disciples about "the leaven" of the Pharisees and Sadducees
(Matt. 16:6, 12).

The early Christians surely believed in the completeness of
Jesus's saving work. Peter received courage to confess before the
Jewish council that "there is salvation in no one else, for there is
no other name under heaven given among men by which we must
be saved" (Acts 4:12). We have read frequently in Paul's writings
that we are saved by pure grace. The apostle brought that gospel
in purity. We can observe that in all of his letters. But by means
of his letter to the Galatians, the apostle provided us with an
unsurpassable lesson regarding Christ's mediatorial work.

Just like most of us, the Galatians were of Gentile descent
(they were possibly Celts). From Paul they had received the gospel of Jesus Christ, who was crucified in the place of sinners, and
they had believed that they were also children of Abraham, even
though they had not one drop of Jewish blood flowing through
their veins. With that development, the time of shadows was
past, including circumcision, sacrifices, keeping the Sabbath,
and the like. What survived was simply this: Believe in the Lord
Jesus Christ!

But after Paul departed from Galatia, other preachers entered
the region of Galatia and contradicted the apostle in a mean-
spirited way. Could Gentiles become children of God simply by
believing in Christ and nothing more? No, that had to be supplemented with keeping all the regulations that govern our Jewish
world, they said. For we have also believed in Jesus as Messiah,
but we have remained Jews. In this way those false teachers were
trying to compel the Galatian Christians to construct their salvation in terms of a mathematical equation: the Jewish law (as they
called it) + Christ = salvation.

When Paul heard what the false teachers in Galatia had
claimed, he cursed both them and their teaching (Gal. 1:8–9). If
you dare to construct your salvation on the basis of a mathematical equation (Christ + the law), then Christ is of absolutely no
benefit any longer (Gal. 5:2). Then you have lost Christ. Then
you are without grace (Gal. 5:4).

From Paul's letter to the Galatians, as well as from his other letters, like Romans and Philippians, we learn clearly that our righteousness before God must not be expected either in whole or in part from ourselves, but exclusively from Christ. People call the contrary, false teaching "Judaizing." This false piety is accursed by Holy Scripture.

Nevertheless, in later centuries it was as though the apostle Paul had never written his letters. In the Middle Ages the gospel was pushed aside by various human doctrines and replaced by the notorious Roman Catholic church teaching. When Luther and others returned to the simple gospel—of Jesus Christ and him crucified—that return frequently cost them their lives (by being burned at the stake). People call this the Reformation.

Let us notice carefully that the teaching of the Reformation ascribes perfect faith to no one else besides Jesus Christ (see Heb. 12:2). Paul did not think he was perfect, but sighed deeply, "Wretched man that I am!" (Rom. 7:24).

Q&A 63

Q. But do our good works earn nothing, even though God promises to reward them in this life and the next?

A. This reward is not earned; it is a gift of grace.

Indeed, no one can deny that Scripture talks about believers' good works and about God rewarding them. Listen to Jesus tell his disciples in the Sermon on the Mount: "In the same way, let your light shine before others, so that they may see your good works and give glory to your Father who is in heaven" (Matt. 5:16). Shortly before this he says, "Blessed are you when others revile you and persecute you and utter all kinds of evil against you falsely on my account. Rejoice and be glad, for your reward is great in heaven, for so they persecuted the prophets who were before you" (Matt. 5:11–12). In connection with giving alms, praying, and fasting in secret, he promises, "And your Father who sees in secret will reward you" (Matt. 6:4, 6, 18). We must love our enemies, just as God does (Luke 6:35).

Indeed, Scripture talks frequently about our good works and their reward. But concerning those good works Scripture also teaches us that God is our Creator, so that the question is legitimate, "Who has given a gift to him that he might be repaid?" (Rom. 11:35). We are children of Adam and have been received by God in grace (Rom. 3:25–26), for the sake of Christ. If we do good works, then we do them out of faith, and we owe that faith to the Holy Spirit. When God rewards our good works, he is thereby crowning his own work.

Let us not be afraid of supposedly "Roman Catholic" Bible verses. They don't exist. The apostle John saw in a vision that the redeemed, upon arriving in glory, take the crowns from their heads and lay them down before the throne of God (Rev. 4:10).

Q&A 64

Q. *Does this teaching not make people careless and wicked?*

A. No. It is impossible that those grafted into Christ by true faith should not bring forth fruits of thankfulness.

Yet another objection: Isn't all this talk about grace dangerous? Can't this tempt people to laziness and idleness? Doesn't it make people careless?

This objection loses sight of the proper relationship between Christ and believers, which functions like that between a head and its body. The body is led by the head, and in the same way true believers are led by their Head, Jesus Christ. We read what Jesus said to his disciples: "Abide in me, and I in you. As the branch cannot bear fruit by itself, unless it abides in the vine, neither can you, unless you abide in me. I am the vine; you are the branches. Whoever abides in me and I in him, he it is that bears much fruit, for apart from me you can do nothing" (John 15:4–5). Faith without works is dead (Jas. 2:26).

Scripture References

Proverbs 20:9
> Who can say, "I have made my heart pure;
> I am clean from my sin"?

Matthew 5:16
"In the same way, let your light shine before others, so that they may see your good works and give glory to your Father who is in heaven."

James 1:19–2:26
Know this, my beloved brothers: let every person be quick to hear, slow to speak, slow to anger; for the anger of man does not produce the righteousness of God. Therefore put away all filthiness and rampant wickedness and receive with meekness the implanted word, which is able to save your souls.

But be doers of the word, and not hearers only, deceiving yourselves. For if anyone is a hearer of the word and not a doer, he is like a man who looks intently at his natural face in a mirror. For he looks at himself and goes away and at once forgets what he was like. But the one who looks into the perfect law, the law of liberty, and perseveres, being no hearer who forgets but a doer who acts, he will be blessed in his doing.

If anyone thinks he is religious and does not bridle his tongue but deceives his heart, this person's religion is worthless. Religion that is pure and undefiled before God, the Father, is this: to visit orphans and widows in their affliction, and to keep oneself unstained from the world.

My brothers, show no partiality as you hold the faith in our Lord Jesus Christ, the Lord of glory. For if a man wearing a gold ring and fine clothing comes into your assembly, and a poor man in shabby clothing also comes in, and if you pay attention to the one who wears the fine clothing and say, "You sit here in a good place," while you say to the poor man, "You stand over there," or, "Sit down at my feet," have you not then made distinctions among yourselves and become judges with evil thoughts? Listen, my beloved brothers, has not God chosen those who are poor in the world to be rich in faith and heirs of the kingdom, which he has promised to those who love him? But you have dishonored the poor man. Are not the rich the ones who oppress you, and the ones who drag you into court? Are they not the ones who blaspheme the honorable name by which you were called?

If you really fulfill the royal law according to the Scripture, "You shall love your neighbor as yourself," you are doing well. But if you show partiality, you are committing sin and are convicted by the law as transgressors. For whoever keeps the whole law but fails in one point has become accountable for all of it. For he who said, "Do not commit adultery," also said, "Do not murder." If you do not commit adultery but do murder, you have become a transgressor of the law. So speak and so act as those who are to be judged under the law of liberty. For judgment is without mercy to one who has shown no mercy. Mercy triumphs over judgment. What good is it, my brothers, if someone says he has faith but does not have works? Can that faith save him? If a brother or sister is poorly clothed and lacking in daily food, and one of you says to them, "Go in peace, be warmed and filled," without giving them the things needed for the body, what good is that? So also faith by itself, if it does not have works, is dead.

But someone will say, "You have faith and I have works." Show me your faith apart from your works, and I will show you my faith by my works. You believe that God is one; you do well. Even the demons believe—and shudder! Do you want to be shown, you foolish person, that faith apart from works is useless? Was not Abraham our father justified by works when he offered up his son Isaac on the altar? You see that faith was active along with his works, and faith was completed by his works; and the Scripture was fulfilled that says, "Abraham believed God, and it was counted to him as righteousness"—and he was called a friend of God. You see that a person is justified by works and not by faith alone. And in the same way was not also Rahab the prostitute justified by works when she received the messengers and sent them out by another way? For as the body apart from the spirit is dead, so also faith apart from works is dead.

LORD'S DAY 25

Next comes a rather large section dealing with the sacraments (Lord's Days 25–30; Lord's Day 31 actually belongs in this section as well, since it deals with the keys of the kingdom of heaven). But first, Lord's Day 25 deals with both sacraments in general, namely, baptism and the Lord's Supper, followed by Lord's Days 26–27, on baptism, and Lord's Days 28–30, on the Lord's Supper.

Q&A 65

Q. *Since then faith alone makes us share in Christ and all his benefits, where does this faith come from?*

A. From the Holy Spirit, who works it in our hearts by the preaching of the gospel, and strengthens it by the use of the sacraments.

To work (in the sense of bringing about) something is different than to strengthen it.

Once the Holy Spirit has worked faith in our hearts, he can make that faith stronger and stronger through the continued preaching of the gospel. Through that repetition of the gospel, faith automatically becomes stronger. But the sacraments are a second kind of means whereby God strengthens our faith as well.

God first used this second kind of means for the benefit of Abraham. In Genesis 17 we read that God laid upon Abraham the obligation of circumcision as the sign of the covenant, something to be performed on his own body and those of his male descendants. Now in the new dispensation, the Holy Spirit has added to instruction in the Word the administration of two sacraments, namely, baptism and the Lord's Supper.

Q&A 66

Q. *What are the sacraments?*

A. The sacraments are holy, visible signs and seals. They were instituted by God so that by their use he might the more fully declare and seal to us the promise of the gospel. And this is the promise: that God graciously grants us forgiveness of sins and everlasting life because of the one sacrifice of Christ accomplished on the cross.

The Latin word *sacramentum* comes from the Roman world. Originally the word referred to the military oath by which soldiers and commanders were bound to each other. The soldiers would serve faithfully under the ensign of their commander. The word *sacramentum* was used very early by Latin-speaking Christians in this sense. With this word they wished to say that martyrs were to stand faithfully in their suffering. This use of the term *sacrament* agrees with what we confess about the covenant of grace. That covenant contains two parts and two parties. God binds himself to us to be our Father, and we are obligated to serve our general, Jesus Christ, God's Son, as faithful soldiers.

The words in Scripture for the sacraments are *sign* and *seal* (Gen. 17:10–11; Rom. 4:11).

A *sign* is used to make something clear, like a traffic sign. Two things are held before us in baptism: first, that we have forgiveness of sins through the blood of Christ, and second, that our life is renewed by the Holy Spirit. These things are invisible. No one can see the forgiveness of sins by the blood of Christ. We obtain this through faith, as a matter of our heart. Nor can anyone see the renewing of our heart, something we obtain as the fruit of faith. These are two invisible realities. But our good God makes them visible to us, for he uses the water of baptism to represent our cleansing both through the blood and through the Spirit of Christ.

What is the purpose of a *seal*? Think of a seal used with a document or decree, or attached to a product. A seal is used to guarantee reliability. In the same way, the sacraments are given to us by our patient God in order to assure us of his promises.

The Catechism intentionally mentions that the sacraments are sacred signs and seals. Both of them, baptism and the Lord's Supper, have been given to us by God himself. He has given no more than these. The Roman Catholics have seven sacraments, five in addition to the ones we recognize. But Scripture does not say anything about these others as sacraments.

Q&A 67

Q. *Are both the Word and the sacraments then intended to focus our faith on the sacrifice of Jesus Christ on the cross as the only ground of our salvation?*

A. Yes, indeed. The Holy Spirit teaches us in the gospel and assures us by the sacraments that our entire salvation rests on Christ's one sacrifice for us on the cross.

It is not difficult to explain the proper relationship between God's Word and the sacraments.

Scripture always places God's Word in front. It pleases the Holy Spirit to incline our hearts to the fear of the Lord by the preaching of the divine Word. Hereby he teaches us to expect our salvation from Jesus alone.

The sacraments follow. They are added to the Word. So they can be used only by people who have learned to believe in the Word. Therefore Jesus commanded his disciples: first teach and then baptize (Matt. 28:19; Mark 16:16). The same applies to the Lord's Supper. Paul commanded that it would benefit a person only after one had examined oneself. To do that, it was necessary to know who Christ was and what he had done (1 Cor. 11:28).

When we say that the sacraments were merely added to the Word and occupy a place of service, that in no way means that we are despising the sacraments. This will become evident in what follows.

Q&A 68

Q. *How many sacraments has Christ instituted in the new covenant?*

A. Two: holy baptism and the holy supper.

The following Lord's Days will deal with baptism and the Lord's Supper separately, for we can observe clear differences between baptism and the Lord's Supper. But their correspondence is also rather significant. This explains why the way the Catechism discusses baptism is at points verbally identical to the way it discusses the Lord's Supper.

We can illustrate this with a few terms.

1. *Word and sacrament.* You could compare the relationship between these two terms with the relationship between a word and an accent mark on that word. Apart from the word, the accent mark tells us nothing. In the same way, we should never separate the sacraments as "accent marks" from the gospel of Jesus's suffering and death for us.

2. *Receive and use.* The Anabaptists thought that no one had a right to be baptized unless he first truly believed. You cannot require that of a child, which explains their view that children should not be baptized.

The mistake in this line of reasoning consists in ignoring the reality that God grants his covenant to believers and their seed. You can see this in the story of Abraham (Gen. 17).

We may not prevent anyone—including a child—from exercising their right to the sacraments. There are many indications that in earlier centuries the Lord's Supper was celebrated even by children.

LORD'S DAY 26

We may speak, then, of one "promise of the gospel," namely, that on account of the one sacrifice of Christ rendered on the cross, God grants us forgiveness of sins and eternal life by grace alone. But to help us better understand and accept this promise, he has supplemented it with two sacraments: baptism and the Lord's Supper.

Q&A 69

Q. How does holy baptism signify and seal to you that the one sacrifice of Christ on the cross benefits you?

A. In this way: Christ instituted this outward washing and with it gave the promise that, as surely as water washes away the dirt from the body, so certainly his blood and Spirit wash away the impurity of my soul, that is, all my sins.

First, baptism was given to us for instruction. It resembles a painting or drawing. No school would be without a large board on the wall, an indispensable aid for teachers to clarify the spoken word. That is what baptism does.

Additionally, baptism was given for sealing, for certifying the promise of the gospel. Let us Christians pay careful attention to this. When someone like us, who has been baptized and is thus washed by the blood of Christ, tramples upon this blood, that person will experience the wrath of God's covenant (Heb. 10:26–31).

This explains why the Catechism here is defending for us the right to confess that I may be just as certain that I have been washed inwardly by the blood and Spirit of Christ as I am that I have been washed outwardly by the water of baptism.

Q&A 70

Q. *What does it mean to be washed with Christ's blood and Spirit?*

A. To be washed with Christ's blood means to receive forgiveness of sins from God, through grace, because of Christ's blood, poured out for us in his sacrifice on the cross. To be washed with his Spirit means to be renewed by the Holy Spirit and sanctified to be members of Christ, so that more and more we become dead to sin and lead a holy and blameless life.

We read in various Scripture passages that Christ shed his blood on the cross for the forgiveness of our sins (Eph. 1:7; Heb. 9:12; 1 John 1:7; Rev. 1:5). But we also read in various Scripture passages that Christ has poured out his Spirit upon the church and that this Spirit brings us to the faith whereby our heart and life are cleansed and renewed (see Acts 2:33; 15:8–9; 22:16; Eph. 2:1–2).

By carefully noting that the Catechism speaks of these two benefits as though they were one, we understand that the Catechism is talking about a twofold cleansing in terms of one washing, a washing through Christ's blood and Spirit (Ezek. 36:25; Joel 2:28; Mark 1:8; John 1:33; 3:5; 1 Cor. 6:11). We just mentioned a twofold benefit distinct from baptism. If there were no baptism, the benefits mentioned would be granted to us just as much in God's promise of the gospel. But now looking back, we can better understand Question and Answer 69. We see that our baptism provides a clear representation of the work that Christ did and does for us and in us. For something that is invisible (the forgiveness of our sins and the renewing of our heart) is presented visually through baptism.

Q&A 71

Q. *Where has Christ promised that he will wash us with his blood and Spirit as surely as we are washed with the water of baptism?*

A. In the institution of baptism, where he says: Go therefore and make disciples of all nations, baptizing them in the name of the Father and of the Son and of the Holy Spirit (Matt. 28:19). Whoever believes and is baptized will be saved, but whoever does not believe will be condemned (Mark 16:16). This promise is repeated where Scripture calls baptism the washing of rebirth and the washing away of sins (Titus 3:5; Acts 22:16).

The Catechism answers this question by referring to a number of Scripture passages: Matthew 28:19; Mark 16:16; Acts 22:16; and Titus 3:5. It could have mentioned Romans 6:3; Colossians 2:11–12; and 1 Peter 3:21 as well. We offer a brief discussion of each.

Matthew 28:19: "Go therefore and make disciples of all nations [or Gentiles], baptizing them in the name of the Father and of the Son and of the Holy Spirit." Now, with the inclusion of the entire populated world, the ancient promise of God given to Abraham in his covenant was being fulfilled (Gen. 12:3; 22:18; Rom. 4:13; Gal. 3:8). Through baptism the Gentiles may be assured that they are covenant members. This is comparable to a young man who chooses a young lady and with his word publicly binds himself to her through marriage. From then on they will be one. She will bear his name, and everything he possesses will be hers as well, including their children. In the same way, we too may now appeal to the fact that we are no longer pagans but children of God.

Mark 16:16: "Whoever believes and is baptized will be saved, but whoever does not believe will be condemned." When the Lord Jesus said these words, he was ready to go back to heaven. Earlier he had given the command to proclaim his gospel in the entire world—not just exclusively to Jewish people but also to Gentiles. For this, the following rule would apply: whoever accepts that gospel will be saved, and whoever rejects it would themselves be rejected.

Acts 22:16: "And now why do you wait? Rise and be baptized and wash away your sins, calling on his name." Paul had sinned against Jesus very gravely. He took pleasure in the death of Stephen. He persecuted followers of Jesus with imprisonment and death. Therefore our Savior humbled him deeply. He afflicted him with blindness and directed him with curt instructions to go to Damascus, where he would hear more about this. For three days Paul did not eat or drink. Then he received a vision in which he saw that someone was addressing him in a friendly manner. This actually happened later. Ananias laid his hand on Paul's head, and Paul received his sight again. To relieve him of his fear, Ananias said, "Come, Saul," which was the apostle's Jewish name, "don't doubt Jesus's willingness to forgive any longer. From now on you are our brother. Arise, receive baptism for the washing away of your sins as you call upon his name." What powerful and concise faith-language on the part of Ananias! For actually, Paul had already received forgiveness, so in this way Paul's despondency was driven back even further.

Romans 6:3: "Do you not know that all of us who have been baptized into Christ Jesus were baptized into his death?" Here the apostle is responding to dishonest accusations about him that were circulating in the Jewish world. Some said he was preaching that people should live carelessly, since they would then receive more grace for forgiveness.

This blasphemy is being opposed here: "How can we who died to sin continue to live in it?" Should those who have died to sin, as we Christians have, be able to continue having anything to do with sin? That doesn't fit with Christian baptism. Whoever has accepted Christ as his Savior and has been baptized according to Christ's command may believe with certainty that his relationship with sin is finished and must be finished. Little wonder that Paul appealed to Christian baptism when people accused him that his preaching of pure grace promoted living in sin. But of course it did not—precisely the opposite. *How can we remain good friends with something that brought our beloved Savior to the cross?*

Galatians 3:26–27: "For in Christ Jesus you are all sons of God, through faith. For as many of you as were baptized into Christ have put on Christ." The Galatians to whom the apostle Paul was writing were converted to Christ through him. But after his departure, other preachers arrived who said that getting saved doesn't happen that easily. They said people must still obey the ancient Jewish laws, such as the requirement of circumcision. When Paul heard that, he wrote, "O foolish Galatians! Who has bewitched you?" (Gal. 3:1). But then he helped them get it right. They were Christians apart from keeping the ancient Mosaic laws, just as Abraham was. Have you been baptized? Then just as certainly you are a Christian with full rights. This is how Paul straightened out the Judaizers who were meddling with the rights of the Galatian Christians.

Titus 3:4–5: "But when the goodness and loving kindness of God our Savior appeared, he saved us, not because of works done by us in righteousness, but according to his own mercy, by the washing of regeneration and renewal of the Holy Spirit." Titus was left behind on the island of Crete to arrange things that still needed improvement (Titus 1:5). Formerly the Cretans had lived like pagans. But the Holy Spirit saved them through the gospel and cleansed them from their paganism. (Just as the Ephesians had first been dead in sin. And just as Paul had earlier been a Pharisee practicing his self-directed piety. That is why Paul speaks of "we.") They were cleansed through the washing of the divine Word. For through the Word, God's Spirit brings us to faith, and this faith regenerates us—it transforms our life into a new life and sets us free from the slavery of sin. Therefore when using the English word *regeneration*, don't think simply of something that happens in the flash of a moment. Ancient Dutch Bible commentators understood verse 5 to be referring to "stages" of our regeneration, which fits better with the Greek word.

1 Peter 3:21: "Baptism, which corresponds to this [that is, the ark], now saves you, not as a removal of dirt from the body but as an appeal to God for a good conscience, through the resurrection of Jesus Christ." The recipients of Peter's first letter were being comforted amid their persecution. Now that they no longer participated in pagan life, they were facing trouble. Through their baptism they were spurred to live henceforth in purity.

Colossians 2:11–12: "In him also you were circumcised with a circumcision made without hands, by putting off the body of the flesh, by the circumcision of Christ, having been buried with him in baptism. . . ." Just like the Ephesians, the Colossians had also been pagans, but they now lived in fellowship with Christ. Nevertheless, false teachers had come to them as well, arguing that they ought to continue living according to the Jewish views regarding, for example, circumcision. But Paul wrote to them: "You have already been circumcised, in the Christian manner, through baptism. Through his Spirit and Word God has put to death your flesh, your old nature, and made you alive in the fellowship of faith together with Christ. When you were subsequently baptized, that baptism was your assurance that just as Christ had dealt with sin through his death and burial, so too you had broken with your sinful past."

LORD'S DAY 27

Q&A 72

Q. *Does this outward washing with water itself wash away sins?*

A. No, only the blood of Jesus Christ and the Holy Spirit cleanse us from all sins.

Roman Catholics argue that unbaptized children cannot be saved. This explains their haste, when a newborn is at risk of dying, to have the baby quickly baptized by the priest or, if necessary, by a doctor or nurse ("emergency baptism").

It is, of course, very disrespectful when some parents wait for weeks, sometimes months, before presenting their child for baptism. But baptism is not indispensable for salvation. Recall the murderer on the cross. We read as well that Cornelius, Lydia, the Ethiopian, and others feared God before their baptism. Let us beware of idolizing the water of baptism.

Q&A 73

Q. *Why then does the Holy Spirit call baptism the washing of regeneration and the washing away of sins?*

A. God speaks in this way for a good reason. He wants to teach us that the blood and Spirit of Christ remove our sins just as water takes away dirt from the body. But, even more important, he wants to assure us by this divine pledge and sign that we are as truly cleansed from our sins spiritually as we are bodily washed with water.

For what reason did the Holy Spirit repeatedly state so concisely in his book, the Holy Scripture, that baptism is just like the washing away of sins and the washing of regeneration itself?

There are two reasons, which are very close to one another.

We discussed the first reason earlier. Baptism is a sign, just as someone in the world of art can point to a painting and talk about "that orchard there" or "this farm," when in fact people are looking simply at a canvas. So too Ananias told Paul that he had to have his sins washed away by being baptized. Baptism as a sign is not far removed from baptism as a seal.

For baptism not only makes the work of Christ and of the Holy Spirit clear and instructive, but it is also a guarantee, a seal that certifies. In his Word God grants us a genuine share in Christ's blood and Spirit and therefore assures us of this so truthfully that anyone who later turns his back on the Christian faith would be trampling upon the blood and Spirit of Christ (Heb. 10:22, 29). Here we are dealing with the same manner of thinking and speaking as in 1 Corinthians 11:17–34, where the apostle writes that anyone who treats the bread and wine of the Lord's Supper in a sinful manner renders himself guilty of nothing less than the body and blood of our Savior. We must take to heart the strong language of Lord's Days 26 and 27, and follow it. As surely as the water of baptism has flowed over me, so surely has Christ cleansed me by his blood and Spirit, and will continue to do so as I get older, as often as I appeal to him in prayer on the basis of my baptism.

Q&A 74

Q. *Should infants, too, be baptized?*

A. Yes. Infants as well as adults belong to God's covenant and congregation. Through Christ's blood the redemption from sin and the Holy Spirit, who works faith, are promised to them no less than to adults. Therefore, by baptism, as sign of the covenant, they must be incorporated into the Christian church and distinguished from the children of unbelievers. This was done in the old covenant by circumcision, in place of which baptism was instituted in the new covenant.

According to the Anabaptists, children may not be baptized, for the Savior did say, "Whoever believes and is baptized will be saved" (Mark 16:16). Therefore, according to them, a person who was baptized as a child and became a believer or gave evidence of believing as an adult should be baptized again. Baptized again— which explains their name, Ana-baptists, since the Greek word *ana* means "again."

The Catechism maintains the threefold right of children of Christians.

First, Christian children are just as much members of the church as their parents. God promised Abraham that he would be not only his God but also the God of his children (Gen. 17:7; Acts 2:39). When some parents in Israel made their children pass through the fire before idols, God accused them: What have you done with my children? (Ezek. 16:21).

Second, Christian children are just as rich as their parents. When many Israelites were disobedient in the wilderness, they did not receive the promised land, but their children did (see Heb. 3).

Third, Christian children have the right to the centuries-old sign that marked them as different, namely, circumcision, which has now been replaced with baptism, however (Col. 2:11). Through baptism they do not become church members for the first time, but rather they are acknowledged as already being church members.

Scripture References

Genesis 17:14
"Any uncircumcised male who is not circumcised in the flesh of his foreskin shall be cut off from his people; he has broken my covenant."

Numbers 23:9
> "For from the top of the crags I see him,
>   from the hills I behold him;
> behold, a people dwelling alone,
>   and not counting itself among the nations!"

Romans 6:4
We were buried therefore with him by baptism into death, in order that, just as Christ was raised from the dead by the glory of the Father, we too might walk in newness of life.

1 Corinthians 7:14
For the unbelieving husband is made holy because of his wife, and the unbelieving wife is made holy because of her husband. Otherwise your children would be unclean, but as it is, they are holy.

LORD'S DAY 28

I n Lord's Day 25 we observed that we may speak of one "promise of the gospel," namely, that on account of the one sacrifice of Christ completed on the cross, out of grace God grants forgiveness of sins and eternal life, but that God has given us two sacraments whereby he desires to help us better understand that promise and to seal that promise through baptism and the Lord's Supper. The sacraments perform the same service, but each in its own way. Lord's Days 26 and 27 discussed baptism, and now we turn to the Lord's Supper.

Q&A 75

Q. *How does the Lord's Supper signify and seal to you that you share in Christ's one sacrifice on the cross and in all his gifts?*

A. In this way: Christ has commanded me and all believers to eat of this broken bread and drink of this cup in remembrance of him. With this command he gave these promises: First, as surely as I see with my eyes the bread of the Lord broken for me and the cup given to me, so surely was his body offered for me and his blood poured out for me on the cross. Second, as surely as I receive from the hand of the minister and taste with my mouth the bread and the cup of the Lord as sure signs of Christ's body and blood, so surely does he himself nourish and refresh my soul to everlasting life with his crucified body and shed blood.

God's church has confessed (in Lord's Day 25) that the Holy Spirit brings about faith in the heart through the proclamation of the holy gospel. She also confesses that God desires to strengthen her faith by means of the Lord's Supper. If someone should ask, "How does the Lord's Supper do that?" then the church responds, "In this way, that I may use the holy supper according to Christ's own institution as a sign and a seal."

The first by itself is already beautiful. The Lord's Supper is given to us first of all as a representation, in order to teach us, as it were, with a portrait. As bread is broken, so your Savior was broken on the cross. What is as nourishing as bread and as refreshing as wine?

The Lord's Supper was given to us, secondly, as a seal. Jesus "took bread, and when he had given thanks, he broke it and gave it to them, saying, 'This is my body, which is given for you. Do this in remembrance of me.' And likewise the cup after they had eaten, saying, 'This cup that is poured out for you is the new covenant in my blood'" (Luke 22:19–20).

Q&A 76

Q. What does it mean to eat the crucified body of Christ and to drink his shed blood?

A. First, to accept with a believing heart all the suffering and the death of Christ and so receive forgiveness of sins and life eternal. Second, to be united more and more to his sacred body through the Holy Spirit, who lives both in Christ and in us. Therefore, although Christ is in heaven and we are on earth, yet we are flesh of his flesh and bone of his bones, and we forever live and are governed by one Spirit, as the members of our body are by one soul.

For a time, the Jews had high expectations of the Lord Jesus. With five loaves and two fishes he fed a crowd of five thousand (John 6:9–10). That sign indicated that, as the true messiah, such a person could liberate them from the yoke of the Romans. But the Lord Jesus wanted nothing to do with this. In order to make known his real purpose in coming to earth, he called *himself* bread. He would give himself for the life of the world (John 6:51).

At that point the Savior had not yet instituted the Lord's Supper, so we need not always think of that in this context. To eat the flesh of the Lord and to drink his blood means to believe in him and thereby to have eternal life (John 6:53).

Even if the Lord's Supper did not exist, we can answer the question about what it means to eat the crucified body of Christ and to drink his shed blood, by saying that this refers to believing in Christ and thereby receiving forgiveness of sins and regeneration.

But the Lord's Supper presents the invisible in terms of something visible. It is given as a sign and, in addition, as a seal, so that we may say, "Just as surely as I receive the bread from the hand of the minister of the Word, I am eating the crucified body of Christ and drinking his shed blood."

But now the question arises: Where do we find that in Scripture?

Q&A 77

Q. *Where has Christ promised that he will nourish and refresh believers with his body and blood as surely as they eat of this broken bread and drink of this cup?*

A. In the institution of the Lord's Supper: "The Lord Jesus, on the night he was betrayed, took bread, and when he had given thanks, he broke it and said, 'This is my body, which is for you; do this in remembrance of me.' In the same way, after supper he took the cup, saying, 'This cup is the new covenant in my blood; do this, whenever you drink it, in remembrance of me.'"For whenever you eat this bread and drink this cup, you proclaim the Lord's death until he comes" (1 Cor 11:23-26). This promise is repeated by Paul where he says: "Is not the cup of thanksgiving for which we give thanks a participation in the blood of Christ? And is not the bread that we break a participation in the body of Christ? Because there is one loaf, we, who are many, are one body, for we all partake of the one loaf" (1 Cor 10:16, 17).

The Lord's Supper is not a human invention, but of divine origin. It is discussed in the Gospels and in the Epistles.

The Gospels

Matthew 26:26–28: "Now as they were eating, Jesus took bread, and after blessing it broke it and gave it to the disciples, and said, 'Take, eat; this is my body.' And he took a cup, and when he had given thanks he gave it to them, saying, 'Drink of it, all of you, for this is my blood of the covenant, which is poured out for many for the forgiveness of sins'" (see the second passage, Mark 14:22–24, and the third, Luke 22:19–20).

The Savior had just instituted the Lord's Supper in the night when he was betrayed. The shadow-filled dispensation of the covenant of grace would now soon be fulfilled. The bread and wine do not change into Christ's body and blood, as the Roman Catholic Church teaches. After all, the Lord was still alive with his disciples when he spoke the words of the Lord's Supper.

The Epistles

We read, for example, the following:

1 Corinthians 10:14–22: From this Scripture passage we may learn that our conduct may not be harmful to others, because as Christians, as congregation, we form one body. You cannot drink the cup of the Lord and the cup of the evil spirits. You cannot have fellowship at the table of the Lord and at the table of demons.

1 Corinthians 11:20–34: The early Christians celebrated the Lord's Supper as part of their so-called love feasts. But it would happen that a rich person brought a lot of provisions for the meal, while a poor person had little or nothing. Paul had to scold the church in Corinth because little groups had apparently formed of church members who were rich and could bring many provisions to eat, while they had little or nothing left over for the needy. The apostle wrote that if someone wanted to indulge in that way, they could better do that at home. At the institution of the Lord's Supper the Lord Jesus had taken only one loaf of bread in his hand. People needed to remember that anyone who celebrates the Lord's Supper in an unworthy manner thereby sins against the body and blood of the Lord. This is not simply everyday food and drink, but consecrated food and drink. Egoism and the Lord's Supper are mutually exclusive.

LORD'S DAY 29

Q&A 78

Q. *Are then the bread and wine changed into the real body and blood of Christ?*

A. No. Just as the water of baptism is not changed into the blood of Christ and is not the washing away of sins itself but is simply God's sign and pledge, so also the bread in the Lord's Supper does not become the body of Christ itself, although it is called Christ's body in keeping with the nature and usage of sacraments.

The Roman Catholic Church teaches that when the priest says the words "For this is my body" (the consecration of the host), then transubstantiation occurs. They mean that the "substance" or the "essence" of the bread and wine changes into the Lord Jesus, but that the properties of the bread and wine, such as taste, smell, form, and perishability, continue to exist. In defense of this claim, they appeal to the fact that several times the Lord Jesus called himself bread, but are we to suppose then, on the basis of other statements of Christ, such as "I am the door," "I am the way," and "I am the true vine" (found in John 10:9; 14:6; 15:1), that he was changed into a door, a way, a stone, a vine, or the like?

Even Luther, the man who wanted nothing to do with the theory of transubstantiation, continued to believe that as soon as the consecration of the host occurred, bread and wine remained bread and wine, but Christ's body was present in, under, and through the bread. This Lutheran teaching about the Lord's Supper is called consubstantiation. If it were correct, Christ would still be on earth today. But Scripture teaches that Christ ascended physically to heaven.

Q&A 79

Q. *Why then does Christ call the bread his body and the cup his blood, or the new covenant in his blood, and why does Paul speak of a participation in the body and blood of Christ?*

A. Christ speaks in this way for a good reason: He wants to teach us by his supper that as bread and wine sustain us in this temporal life, so his crucified body and shed blood are true food and drink for our souls to eternal life. But, even more important, he wants to assure us by this visible sign and pledge, first, that through the working of the Holy Spirit we share in his true body and blood as surely as we receive with our mouth these holy signs in remembrance of him, and, second, that all his suffering and obedience are as certainly ours as if we personally had suffered and paid for our sins.

The Lord's Supper is a sign and a seal. Anyone who keeps that in mind has no need for transubstantiation or consubstantiation. For we have no trouble talking about a painting portraying a farm scene by saying, "I bought that farm on the last day of the museum sale."

Is it then so strange for the Holy Spirit to employ our ordinary manner of speaking, so that just as with baptism, so with the Lord's Supper, he gives to the *sign* (such as the bread, for example) the name of what it represents and of what it points to (namely, the body of the Lord)? For the Lord's Supper, just like baptism, is a painting, as it were, whereby the Holy Spirit makes visible for us what is of course invisible.

Our forgiveness of sins through Christ's suffering and death is an invisible thing. But it is represented in an unsurpassably clear manner through the bread that is broken into pieces, and through the wine that sometimes looks like blood. Paul speaks of this with the words "In the night when he was betrayed." With what other means do we obtain such intimate communion as we do with eating and drinking?

A *sign* is provided in order to clarify, and a *seal* in order to convince. The Lord Jesus knew that his beloved disciples were but people with blemishes, also in their faith. Paul used that way of speaking to explain concerning Christ: "This is my body that is given for you; do this in remembrance of me," and later with the words, "Drink of it, all of you, for this is the blood of my covenant that was shed unto a complete remission of sins." We may know for sure that the proper foundation was laid there at Golgotha for the forgiveness of sins for all times.

We are placed in communion with Jesus not only when we celebrate the Lord's Supper reverently. Being placed in communion with Jesus happened already when God's Spirit taught us to believe in him by accepting the gospel (a communion of faith)—indeed, it happened even earlier (as a communion of promise), already at our baptism. Through our believing celebration of the Lord's Supper, that communion is not being brought about for the first time, but is being deepened and strengthened.

LORD'S DAY 30

Q. *What difference is there between the Lord's Supper and the papal mass?*

A. The Lord's Supper testifies to us, first, that we have complete forgiveness of all our sins through the one sacrifice of Jesus Christ, which he himself accomplished on the cross once for all; and, second, that through the Holy Spirit we are grafted into Christ who with his true body is now in heaven at the right hand of the Father, and this is where he wants to be worshiped. But the mass teaches, first, that the living and the dead do not have forgiveness of sins through the suffering of Christ unless he is still offered for them daily by the priests; and, second, that Christ is bodily present in the form of bread and wine, and there is to be worshiped. Therefore the mass is basically nothing but a denial of the one sacrifice and suffering of Jesus Christ, and an accursed idolatry.

Our Catechism currently has 129 questions and answers. But the first edition of this instruction manual contained only 128 questions and answers. In the second edition, published in 1563, this 80th Question and Answer was included, presumably because the Council of Trent had strongly condemned the Reformed a short time before.

The word *mass* is an abbreviated form of the Latin word *missa*, which means "to be sent away," "to leave." In ancient times the Lord's Supper was celebrated only at the end of the worship service, and unbelievers had to leave.

According to the Roman Catholic Church, the mass is a sacrifice (in Latin, *hostia*) offered to God after bread and wine have been changed into the body and blood of Christ. This sacrifice can occur on behalf of those present as well as those absent, who are traveling or who have died, or those who are in purgatory. But Scripture doesn't say a word either about such a thing as purgatory or about a continuing sacrifice. Christ made satisfaction with one single offering for all time (Heb. 10:12; 1 Pet. 3:18). If there are extra wafers after the mass has been concluded, they are treated carefully; some Roman Catholic men remove their hats when they pass by a church that has the consecrated host, for they believe that this consecrated host is Christ. Roman Catholics genuflect when entering the church. But Scripture says that we are to worship the Lord our God and serve him only (Matt. 4:10).

Q&A 81

Q. Who are to come to the table of the Lord?

A. Those who are truly displeased with themselves because of their sins and yet trust that these are forgiven them and that their remaining weakness is covered by the suffering and death of Christ, and who also desire more and more to strengthen their faith and amend their life. But hypocrites and those who do not repent eat and drink judgment upon themselves.

Q&A 82

Q. *Are those also to be admitted to the Lord's Supper who by their confession and life show that they are unbelieving and ungodly?*

A. No, for then the covenant of God would be profaned and his wrath kindled against the whole congregation. Therefore, according to the command of Christ and his apostles, the Christian church is duty bound to exclude such persons by the keys of the kingdom of heaven, until they amend their lives.

Celebrating the Lord's Supper was commanded by Christ and his apostles. Jesus said, "Do this in remembrance of me" (Luke 22:19). Because most Christians were baptized in early youth, in due time they were supposed to participate with their parents in celebrating the Lord's Supper. When should they begin doing that? We find no age for that mentioned anywhere in the Bible. Reports from the early centuries of Christianity indicate that already at that time very young children participated, but later it became customary for the children to be instructed more deeply. Perhaps this happened under the influence of the well-known command for self-examination that Paul provides in 1 Corinthians 11:28–29: "Let a person examine himself, then, and so eat of the bread and drink of the cup. For anyone who eats and drinks without discerning the body eats and drinks judgment on himself." A child can be too young for such self-examination.

Unbelievers may not celebrate the Lord's Supper. In Scripture we read that in some periods of history there were many unbelievers in the church: in the wilderness, in the period of the judges, in Jeremiah's time, when Jesus was not accepted by "his own" (John 1:11), and when false brothers crept into the church (Gal. 2:4). But not all periods are alike. Under Joshua things in the church were better than under Moses. Not all churches are alike. The Lord Jesus scolded the church of Laodicea very severely, but not the churches of Smyrna and Philadelphia. So let us be careful, and recall the possibility of these three kinds of church members:

1. In the past and present there were and are certainly church members who desire to serve their heavenly Father reverently according to his covenant and his Word. When the church of the old dispensation repeatedly forsook God's covenant, she was punished with captivity and Jerusalem was destroyed. When some church members in Corinth treated the Lord's Supper profanely, God visited them with sickness and death (1 Cor. 11:30).

Nevertheless we must understand these words properly. In 1 Corinthians 11, the apostle Paul did not intend the requirement of self-examination to demand that before every celebration of the Lord's Supper one must wonder whether or not he belonged to Christ's church. But rather, one must reflect on the manner in which one was celebrating the Lord's Supper, namely, in a worthy manner, which means without mutual animosity and without pride. With many celebrations of the Lord's Supper, we are ashamed because our deep guilt made necessary this bitter suffering of God's Son. So we occasionally must honestly acknowledge that we have many deficiencies. Paul wrote, "Wretched man that I am!" (Rom. 7:24), and acknowledged that he had been saved in hope (Rom. 8:24). But his course of life was good and Christ continued as his Intercessor (Rom. 8:34) even now (1 Pet. 1:4–5; 1 John 1:7; Heb. 4:15).

2. Some church members do not fear God in truth and still behave piously. In Scripture they are called hypocrites, from a Greek word for play actor (Matt. 6:2; Mark 7:6). In Isaiah's day, God the Lord complained about disobedient religion (Isa. 1; Jer. 7). We also read about "false apostles." It is impossible, however, to identify such members.

3. We can identify those church members who publicly misbehave, and conduct that takes various forms, like teaching that completely contradicts Scripture, or ignoring God's commandments.

When God's covenant is publicly violated, the church must not close her eyes to that, for example, out of laziness. God refused to tolerate negligence with regard to his sacrament of circumcision even on the part of Moses, but almost punished him with death (Exod. 4:24–26). In Corinth, God punished church members on account of disrespect toward the Lord's Supper. Would we openly tolerate such a sin? No, the church must not neglect employing the keys of the kingdom in response to those who sin publicly and impenitently. See our further discussion of Lord's Day 31.

Scripture References

John 6:35
Jesus said to them, "I am the bread of life; whoever comes to me shall not hunger, and whoever believes in me shall never thirst."

John 6:54–55
"Whoever feeds on my flesh and drinks my blood has eternal life, and I will raise him up on the last day. For my flesh is true food, and my blood is true drink."

John 6:59
Jesus said these things in the synagogue, as he taught at Capernaum.

LORD'S DAY 31

Q&A 83

Q. *What are the keys of the kingdom of heaven?*

A. The preaching of the holy gospel and church discipline. By these two the kingdom of heaven is opened to believers and closed to unbelievers.

In Scripture, in addition to the phrase *kingdom of heaven*, another word appears in the same context, for example, in Matthew 8:11–12, where we read both the terms *kingdom* and *kingdom of heaven*. When we later discuss the second petition of the Lord's Prayer (Lord's Day 48), we will observe still greater variation. The phrase *kingdom of heaven* leads us to think immediately of future glory or simply of heaven.

Christ discussed earnestly with his disciples the matter of entering heaven, and gave them authority regarding that. That is why the Catechism speaks of "keys" of the kingdom of heaven. In order to understand that term, we need to reflect on the following passages.

Matthew 16:19: "I will give you the keys of the kingdom of heaven, and whatever you bind on earth shall be bound in heaven, and whatever you loose on earth shall be loosed in heaven."

We know that in the time of Jesus, a view was prevalent among the Jewish people that the messiah would deliver them from the Romans. That is why in many places Jesus gathered a significant following on account of his miracles, but later he no longer satisfied the desires of the people, nor did he fulfill their wishes. Therefore Jesus asked his disciples, "Who do you say that I am?" Peter answered that he was the Messiah, the Son of the living God. Jesus explained Peter's answer as something given him by Jesus's Father himself. He went on to say, "You are Peter [rock], and on this rock I will build my church, and the gates [power] of hell shall not prevail against it. I will give you the keys of the kingdom of heaven, and whatever you bind on earth shall be bound in heaven, and whatever you loose on earth shall be loosed in heaven" (Matt. 16:15–19).

Peter did a lot in terms of bringing many people to the church. Recall the great day of Pentecost. The Roman Catholic Church is entirely mistaken, however, in making Peter out to be its first pope, since he was not. The other disciples received the same promise from Jesus that Peter did, something that becomes evident from the next passages.

Matthew 18:15–18: "If your brother sins against you, go and tell him his fault, between you and him alone. If he listens to you, you have gained your brother. But if he does not listen, take one or two others along with you, that every charge may be established by the evidence of two or three witnesses. If he refuses to listen to them, tell it to the church. And if he refuses to listen even to the church, let him be to you as a Gentile and a tax collector. Truly, I say to you, whatever you bind on earth shall be bound in heaven, and whatever you loose on earth shall be loosed in heaven."

From Mark 9 it is evident that Jesus spoke these words to the disciples because they were quarreling among themselves about who among them was first. Jesus took a small child and placed him in their midst, and said, "Truly, I say to you, unless you turn and become like children, you will never enter the kingdom of heaven" (Matt. 18:3).

When the Lord Jesus would later depart, he would entrust to the disciples the care of the church: "If your brother sins against you, go and tell him his fault, between you and him alone" (Matt. 18:15). If he does not listen, one should take one or two others along, so that the matter may be established with the testimony of two or three witnesses. If he continues not to listen, one should tell the church, whereby Jesus meant those who govern the church, namely, the elders (Acts 15:2; Phil. 1:1; 1 Tim. 4:14). If he refuses to listen to the church, then he is to be as a pagan and a tax collector. This mandate applied not only to Peter but to all the disciples.

John 20:23: "If you forgive the sins of any, they are forgiven them; if you withhold forgiveness from any, it is withheld."

On the day he rose from the dead, Jesus appeared among his disciples and appointed them to be his substitutes: "As the Father has sent me, even so I am sending you" (John 20:21). From this we get the term *apostle*, which means "sent one." With a view to their task, Jesus said, "Receive the Holy Spirit," referring not to Pentecost but to his imminent departure. During the first evening after he arose, the Savior told his disciples that he would be leaving them with the task of preaching the gospel everywhere. The Gospel writer John tells us that Jesus also said, "If you forgive the sins of any, they are forgiven them; if you withhold forgiveness from any, it is withheld."

Christ appointed his apostles and his church as those holding authority over the entrance to heaven. We must pay careful attention to his commands. Otherwise things can happen as happened with the papal bull—which Luther threw into the fire.

Q&A 84

Q. How is the kingdom of heaven opened and closed by the preaching of the gospel?

A. According to the command of Christ, the kingdom of heaven is opened when it is proclaimed and publicly testified to each and every believer that God has really forgiven all their sins for the sake of Christ's merits, as often as they by true faith accept the promise of the gospel. The kingdom of heaven is closed when it is proclaimed and testified to all unbelievers and hypocrites that the wrath of God and eternal condemnation rest on them as long as they do not repent. According to this testimony of the gospel, God will judge both in this life and in the life to come.

Living and Dying in Joy

By its nature, God's Word is a word of blessing, but whoever despises it will perish along with the wicked world. When God's Son came to earth himself, some church leaders looked down their noses at the ordinary people, and foisted on them their strict rabbinic commands. Jesus said, "But woe to you, scribes and Pharisees, hypocrites! For you shut the kingdom of heaven in people's faces. For you neither enter yourselves nor allow those who would enter to go in" (Matt. 23:13; see also Luke 11:52).

Then God's Son sent out his apostles as preachers among Israel· "The one who hears you hears me" (Luke 10:16). After his death and resurrection Jesus sent his apostles also to the Gentiles. The preaching to the Gentiles included this warning: "Whoever does not believe will be condemned" (Mark 16:16; see also Mark 6:11; John 20:21–23).

The opening of the kingdom of heaven

Paul wrote to the church in Rome that he was hoping to come soon for the sake of his gospel to Jew and Greek (non-Jew). The apostle wrote that a person was not justified on the basis of his own self-produced righteousness, but on the basis of Christ's righteousness (Rom. 1:17; 3:21–26). The other apostles wrote similarly. Even the most upright Christian needs the forgiveness of sins, but also continually needs the blood of Jesus, God's Son, to cleanse us from all sin (1 John 1:7).

Nevertheless, conditions remain that must be satisfied. The apostle Paul wrote that faith comes from hearing the Word of God (Rom. 10:17). For "Christians" who were walking "in the darkness," the key of the gospel did not open but closed the door of the kingdom.

Closing the door of the kingdom

People who know the gospel can reject it by word or conduct, and thereby become all the more guilty. That is what the Lord Jesus said, for example (Matt. 11:20–24; see also John 12:48; 15:22), to the cities of Chorazin, Bethsaida, and Capernaum! "Whoever believes in the Son has eternal life; whoever does not obey the Son shall not see life, but the wrath of God remains on him" (John 3:36). The apostles emphasized to their readers that they ought not to be guilty of rejecting the apostolic preaching. Guard against disobedience to God's Word (Heb. 2:2–3; 10:29–31, 39). The church must also warn against unbelief that despises the first key, the divine Word. The gospel can sometimes be an aroma of death unto death (2 Cor. 2:16).

Q&A 85

Q. How is the kingdom of heaven closed and opened by church discipline?

A. According to the command of Christ, people who call themselves Christians but show themselves to be un-Christian in doctrine or life are first repeatedly admonished in a brotherly manner. If they do not give up their errors or wickedness, they are reported to the church, that is, to the elders. If they do not heed also their admonitions, they are forbidden the use of the sacraments, and they are excluded by the elders from the Christian congregation, and by God himself from the kingdom of Christ. They are again received as members of Christ and of the church when they promise and show real amendment.

Originally the term *discipline* referred to nurture, and only later did it come to refer to punishment. We can discern the content of ecclesiastical discipline in the time of the apostles by considering the notions of their binding and loosing in the following Scripture passages.

The apostle Paul had preached to the Thessalonians that the Christ who had died, arisen, and gone to heaven would one day return in glory. For some, that became the reason for setting aside their daily work. During his stay in Thessalonica, the apostle disapproved of this, but when he subsequently learned of it, he roundly condemned it in his letters to the church. The church had to see to it that she did not come under the influence of that mistaken view and thereby end up setting aside Paul's teaching. That teaching concerning idleness appeared to be godly but was in fact ungodly (2 Thess. 3:11). If those holding that view rejected this Scriptural admonition, then people had to avoid having any contact with them.

In Titus 3 we find another example of excluding people from the church. In this chapter the apostle is warning against deviations not in conduct but in doctrine. On the island of Crete, where Paul had left behind his "son" Titus, there were people who had come under the influence of Jewish and Gnostic false teaching. Such teaching was creating unnecessary problems for people. Paul wrote, "But avoid foolish controversies, genealogies, dissensions, and quarrels about the law, for they are unprofitable and worthless" (Titus 3:9). Titus was called to warn them several times first, but if that proved unsuccessful, he had to reject them and remove them from God's church: "As for a person who stirs up division, after warning him once and then twice, have nothing more to do with him" (Titus 3:10). Other errors surfaced in other places, but these had an appearance of being biblically faithful (Gal. 6:12; Rom. 16:17).

In Corinth a very strange case occurred. A woman had been divorced by her husband, and she married the son of her former husband. Such sexual immorality was rejected even among pagans (1 Cor. 5:1–2). Of course that man had to be severely punished. Why? Naturally, if he did not listen, he had to be put out of the church. But if he repented he had to be heartily received again.

By whom must ecclesiastical discipline be exercised? By the elders together (Matt. 18:17; 1 Tim. 4:14). For what purpose? To save the erring one (Matt. 18:15; 2 Thess. 3:15; 2 Cor. 2:7–8). With what authority? In the name and with the authority of the Lord Jesus Christ (Matt. 16:19; 18:18; 1 Cor. 5:4).

Scripture References

Matthew 16:18–19

"And I tell you, you are Peter, and on this rock I will build my church, and the gates of hell shall not prevail against it. I will give you the keys of the kingdom of heaven, and whatever you bind on earth shall be bound in heaven, and whatever you loose on earth shall be loosed in heaven."

Matthew 18:15–18
"If your brother sins against you, go and tell him his fault, between you and him alone. If he listens to you, you have gained your brother. But if he does not listen, take one or two others along with you, that every charge may be established by the evidence of two or three witnesses. If he refuses to listen to them, tell it to the church. And if he refuses to listen even to the church, let him be to you as a Gentile and a tax collector. Truly, I say to you, whatever you bind on earth shall be bound in heaven, and whatever you loose on earth shall be loosed in heaven."

Luke 11:52
"Woe to you lawyers! For you have taken away the key of knowledge. You did not enter yourselves, and you hindered those who were entering."

LORD'S DAY 32

Q&A 86

Q. *Since we have been delivered from our misery by grace alone through Christ, without any merit of our own, why must we yet do good works?*

A. Because Christ, having redeemed us by his blood, also renews us by his Holy Spirit to be his image, so that with our whole life we may show ourselves thankful to God for his benefits, and he may be praised by us. Further, that we ourselves may be assured of our faith by its fruits, and that by our godly walk of life we may win our neighbors for Christ.

Q&A 87

Q. *Can those be saved who do not turn to God from their ungrateful and impenitent walk of life?*

A. By no means. Scripture says that no unchaste person, idolater, adulterer, thief, greedy person, drunkard, slanderer, robber, or the like shall inherit the kingdom of God.

Lord's Day 32 answers the question as to why we must still do good works. In a way we might summarize as follows:

1. Otherwise God would not be praised through us.
2. Otherwise our faith would not be a certain faith.

3. Otherwise we would not win our neighbor for Christ.

4. Otherwise we would not inherit God's kingdom.

Otherwise God would not be praised through us

Often children resemble their parents, and we hardly think such a phenomenon strange. The same is true when that comparison involves especially spiritual life.

Before his conversion the apostle Paul was a genuine Pharisaic Jew. In his letters he talks frequently about this. For example, his letter to the Ephesians was written to former pagans, to whom he writes as people with a past just like his. As pagans they had been *dead* (Eph. 2:1). But the God of mercy made us *alive* (v. 5).

Nevertheless the apostle goes on to warn the Ephesian Christians against sin and the devil. For otherwise they would grieve the Holy Spirit. Rather, they must be imitators of God (Eph. 5:1); "Let no one deceive you with empty words" (Eph. 5:6); sing to the Lord and rejoice heartily (Eph. 5:19). Everyone in the church was being addressed—including children and parents. God's name must not be blasphemed on our account, but must be honored and praised.

Otherwise our faith would not be a certain faith

We must be careful not to understand the Catechism's language ("that we ourselves may be assured of our faith by its fruits") to mean that we must constantly turn to look at ourselves if we are to dare to conclude that we now have faith, since we have discovered fruit in ourselves: "Now I dare to believe that I am a believer."

For then our faith would rest upon a logical syllogism rather than on the divine leading of our life. For we were born to Christian parents and we are baptized, as proof that we belong to God's covenant people. When our parents teach us to understand what that means, then through that faith we will receive hearts that have been cleansed (Acts 15:9). When Paul was converted from his Jewish self-directed piety, he was no longer a wretch who slavishly sought to keep the law, but he simply took "delight in the law of God" (Rom. 7:22).

Otherwise we would not win our neighbor for Christ

Whenever we Christians not only read and hear God's Word but also do it, then the church is "a letter from Christ," as the apostle Paul writes (2 Cor. 3:3). The apostle commanded that everything done in the church's gatherings be done decently and orderly. The Lord Jesus commanded his disciples: "Love your enemies, do good to those who hate you, bless those who curse you pray for those who abuse you," and much more (see-Luke 6:27–35).

Otherwise we would not inherit God's kingdom

When the apostle perceived that not every Christian in Corinth was honoring the break with their former pagan living, he admonished them sternly in this way: "Or do you not know that the unrighteous will not inherit the kingdom of God? Do not be deceived: neither the sexually immoral, nor idolaters, nor adulterers, nor men who practice homosexuality, nor thieves, nor the greedy, nor drunkards, nor revilers, nor swindlers will inherit the kingdom of God" (1 Cor. 6:9–10).

LORD'S DAY 33

Q&A 88

Q. *What is the true repentance or conversion of man?*

A. It is the dying of the old nature and the coming to life of the new.

It is obvious that the Catechism is going to pay special attention to conversion. For since apart from conversion no one will inherit the kingdom of God, we should know clearly what it is that we must understand by conversion.

Unfortunately, since our Reformed confessions were written, there has been a change in linguistic usage. Formerly the word *conversion* was often used as a synonym of the word *regeneration*. At the Synod of Dort it was particularly customary to speak of "conversion or regeneration." The language of the Belgic Confession (art. 22–24) states that the Holy Spirit regenerates us and makes us new people through faith.

Presumably, by using the equivalent of our word *born* or *birth*, the Dutch translation of Scripture passages like John 3:3; 1 Peter 1:3, 23; and others, gave rise to understanding these words as referring to something that takes only a very brief time, since an ordinary physical birth (of a child) takes only a very short time. Aside from the fact, however, that most often this is not the case, the Greek word used in those passages does not indicate at all something that is momentary, but rather something that lasts for an entire lifetime, or at least for a large part of a lifetime. Our original liturgical Form for Baptism taught clearly that regeneration consists of two parts: first, that we have an upright remorse and sorrow concerning our sin, and that we deny our own understanding and various lusts, and submit ourselves to the will of God; and second, that we begin to have desire and love to live in all holiness and righteousness according to God's Word.

One instructive Scripture passage in this connection is John 3, where we read that the Lord Jesus reprimanded the Pharisee Nicodemus for thinking about regeneration in terms of the birth of a baby. He should have known better from Scripture.

The word *regeneration* does not appear in the Old Testament. From this we can conclude that the Lord Jesus was concerned not with the term but with the matter itself. Why didn't Nicodemus recall God's requirement for Israel: "Circumcise therefore the foreskin of your heart, and be no longer stubborn" (Deut. 10:16)? Or as it says elsewhere, "Cast away from you all the transgressions that you have committed, and make yourselves a new heart and a new spirit! Why will you die, O house of Israel?" (Ezek. 18:31). During the dark period of Isaiah, Jeremiah, and Ezekiel, the Lord promised his disobedient people that in the future he would give them a new heart and a new spirit (Jer. 31:33). The restoration of Israel would be like a resurrection of the dead from the grave (Ezek. 36:26; 37): "For this is the covenant that I will make with the house of Israel after those days, declares the LORD: I will put my law within them, and I will write it on their hearts" (Jer. 31:33). The Messiah would later come to such a humble and God-fearing people, unto the blessing of many Gentiles as well (Isa. 42:1–4; 49:6).

In the New Testament we see that the apostles spoke to Christians who had come from among the Gentiles in the same manner as our Savior had spoken to the Jew Nicodemus. The apostle Paul wrote to the Corinthians that anyone who did not break with his former pagan life would not inherit the kingdom of God. The apostle provided an entire list of sins (1 Cor. 6:10). He wrote similarly to others, such as the Ephesians, "For you may be sure of this, that everyone who is sexually immoral or impure, or who is covetous (that is, an idolater), has no inheritance in the kingdom of Christ and God" (Eph. 5:5).

Anyone reading Holy Scripture attentively will observe that with words and phrases like *conversion*, *renewing*, *regeneration*, and *making alive*, the same thing is in view, so that the church of Christ was fully scriptural in providing a similar description for similar things like regeneration (in the older Form for Baptism) and conversion (here in Lord's Day 33).

This conversion or regeneration consists, to state it briefly, in heartfelt remorse for sin and heartfelt desire and love for fearing God. The Holy Spirit brings about this remorse and this desire through the preaching of the Word, through instruction in the Bible. And fathers and mothers, let us not forget the Christian nurture of our children!

Q&A 89

Q. What is the dying of the old nature?

A. It is to grieve with heartfelt sorrow that we have offended God by our sin, and more and more to hate it and flee from it.

Q&A 90

Q. What is the coming to life of the new nature?

A. It is a heartfelt joy in God through Christ, and a love and delight to live according to the will of God in all good works.

Q&A 91

Q. But what are good works?

A. Only those which are done out of true faith, in accordance with the law of God, and to his glory, and not those based on our own opinion or on precepts of men.

Question and Answer 88 prepared us to learn about genuine or true conversion. In the Bible we also read about false and nongenuine conversion. Recall, for example, the remorse of King Ahab about his murder of Naboth, though he refused to listen to the prophet Micah (1 Kings 21–22). Judas was also remorseful about his betrayal, but he committed suicide (Matt. 27:3–5). But the conversion of David and his remorse over his sin against Uriah and Bathsheba were sincere, and the forgiveness he received is described for our instruction, along with David's prayer, in Psalm 51.

The terms *old man* (or *old nature*) and *new man* (or *new nature*) must not be given any other content than the Bible gives them. We should not understand them to refer to two successive periods of time. After their conversion to the Christian faith, the Ephesians were admonished to put their old nature to death. The Galatians in Bithynia who had become Christians were given the same admonition. We can read about true conversion or regeneration in Romans 6 and Colossians 3 as well.

Unfortunately the danger of sin continues to threaten us until death. As long as we are alive we cannot do without prayer for God's leading through his Word and Spirit. Only in this way will our life please God, a life of good works.

We should not understand good works to refer to extraordinary accomplishments. The Pharisees thought that through their own contrived Sabbath commandments they were honoring God very highly, but our Lord Jesus approved his disciples' plucking grain in a field and eating it on the Sabbath (Matt. 12:1–8). When the Savior had to appear before the Sanhedrin, his works were condemned as evil works rather than good works. Later the preaching of the apostles was opposed behind their backs by Jewish false teachers who claimed that their piety was much better (Acts 26:9; Rom. 6:1; 10:2; Gal. 2:5). Our ancestors rejected the Roman Catholic doctrine of good works at the time of the Reformation. We should not do good works in order to be saved by them, but because God has promised us salvation in the gospel and has assured us of that by our baptism. We must praise that historical course of events with gratitude. You have been given the promise of the gospel so "that you may proclaim the excellencies of him who called you out of darkness into his marvelous light" (1 Pet. 2:9).

Good works simply refer to doing what is good. And God has summarized what is good in the Ten Commandments.

Scripture References

Deuteronomy 10:16
"Circumcise therefore the foreskin of your heart, and be no longer stubborn."

Ezekiel 18:31
"Cast away from you all the transgressions that you have committed, and make yourselves a new heart and a new spirit! Why will you die, O house of Israel?"

Colossians 3:1–14
If then you have been raised with Christ, seek the things that are above, where Christ is, seated at the right hand of God. Set your minds on things that are above, not on things that are on earth. For you have died, and your life is hidden with Christ in God. When Christ who is your life appears, then you also will appear with him in glory.

Put to death therefore what is earthly in you: sexual immorality, impurity, passion, evil desire, and covetousness, which is idolatry. On account of these the wrath of God is coming. In these you too once walked, when you were living in them. But now you must put them all away: anger, wrath, malice, slander, and obscene talk from your mouth. Do not lie to one another, seeing that you have put off the old self with its practices and have put on the new self, which is being renewed in knowledge after the image of its creator. Here there is not Greek and Jew, circumcised and uncircumcised, barbarian, Scythian, slave, free; but Christ is all, and in all.

Put on then, as God's chosen ones, holy and beloved, compassionate hearts, kindness, humility, meekness, and patience, bearing with one another and, if one has a complaint against another, forgiving each other; as the Lord has forgiven you, so you also must forgive. And above all these put on love, which binds everything together in perfect harmony.

LORD'S DAY 34

The word *law* is our English word for the Hebrew word *torah*. This latter word means "instruction" or "teaching." It is regrettable that in the course of time our word *law* has come to be used in a way that has given it a harsh sound. Many people associate the words *law* and *legal* with *legalism*. People speak of a legalistic sermon that fails to sound forth the gospel of God's grace, but was instead an address about justice, wrongdoing, punishment, and the like. But surely we must not ascribe this kind of meaning to the biblical term *law*, because Paul calls the law a guardian (*paidagōgos*) unto Christ (Gal. 3:24). God is not interested in beating us with his law. "His commandments are not burdensome" (1 John 5:3).

The law does not at all exclude every notion of justice and obligation. On the contrary, God governed his ancient people Israel by establishing his covenant in a way that highlighted precisely his rights. In the world of the ancient Near East it was especially customary that a king who reached an agreement with his vassal would remind his vassal near the beginning of the treaty document of all the benefits that he had shown him earlier, to his father, and even to his grandfather. This was called the historical prologue, something we find in Scripture as well, namely, the prologue to the Ten Commandments in Exodus 20: "And God spoke all these words, saying, 'I am the LORD your God, who brought you out of the land of Egypt, out of the house of slavery'" (vv. 1–2). Later, in Deuteronomy 5, Moses once again narrated the establishing of the covenant by repeating the same words: "I am the LORD your God, who brought you out of the land of Egypt, out of the house of slavery" (v. 6)

If we reflect carefully on this situation, we will understand not only why God gave ten commandments to Israel as covenant obligations, but also that the historical prologue included the requirement that Israel would never consort with other gods (idols or non-gods).

Q&A 92

Q. *What is the law of the LORD?*

A. God spoke all these words:
I am the LORD your God, who brought you out of the land of Egypt, out of the house of slavery.

1. You shall have no other gods before me.
2. You shall not make for yourself a carved image, or any likeness of anything that is in heaven above, or that is in the earth beneath, or that is in the water under the earth. You shall not bow down to them or serve them, for I the LORD your God am a jealous God, visiting the iniquity of the fathers on the children to the third and the fourth generation of those who hate me, but showing steadfast love to thousands of those who love me and keep my commandments.
3. You shall not take the name of the LORD your God in vain, for the LORD will not hold him guiltless who takes his name in vain.
4. Remember the Sabbath day, to keep it holy. Six days you shall labor, and do all your work, but the seventh day is a Sabbath to the LORD your God. On it you shall not do any work, you, or your son, or your daughter, your male servant, or your female servant, or your livestock, or the sojourner who is within your gates. For in six days the LORD made heaven and earth, the sea, and all that is in them, and rested on the seventh day. Therefore the LORD blessed the Sabbath day and made it holy.

(continued on next page)

Q&A 92 *(continued)*

5. Honor your father and your mother, that your days may be long in the land the LORD your God is giving you.
6. You shall not murder.
7. You shall not commit adultery.
8. You shall not steal.
9. You shall not give false witness against your neighbor.
10. You shall not covet your neighbor's house; you shall not covet your neighbor's wife, or his male servant, or his female servant, or his ox, or his donkey, or anything that is your neighbor's.

No, we may not contrast the Ten Commandments and the gospel, as though the former were harsh and the latter mild. We encounter this misunderstanding occasionally, for example, with the Pharisees. But the Lord Jesus refused to accept this contrast and called the church back to the freedom enjoyed by God's covenant people due to the covenant with patriarch Abraham. The Lord Jesus said, "Come to me, all who labor and are heavy laden [by the self-invented religion of the Pharisees], and I will give you rest" (Matt. 11:28). He accused the Pharisees of rendering the Word and command of God powerless by means of their fabrications (Matt. 15:6; Mark 7:13). The apostle Paul wrote that when they read the law of Moses, the unbelieving Jews had a veil over their heart (2 Cor. 3:15). In Galatians 3 the apostle called the law a guardian (*paidagōgos*) unto Christ. Therefore we can properly call the law the gospel of the shadows. "Blessed is that nation whose God is the LORD," says Psalm 33:12. When we read the Ten Words carefully, we see that in Exodus 20:1–17, the phrase "Yahweh ["the LORD" in most English translations] your God" appears six times, and in Deuteronomy 5:6–21 it appears nine times. This was a powerful reminder of God's covenant with Israel's forefather Abraham (Gen. 17:1–8). Recall how faithfully those promises had been fulfilled in the course of the centuries, ultimately by means of the coming of Christ as the Savior for Jews and Gentiles. We ourselves have been transferred out of the pagan power of Satan into the kingdom of God's Son (Col. 1:13; 1 Pet. 2:9–10). It is true, now we ought to keep God's covenant out of gratitude. For we are no longer confronted with the entire shadowy law of Moses with its stipulations regarding priests, sacrifices, holy places, holy times, and so on. Those shadows have fallen away. Let no one despise the Old Testament, but we must realize that it can be properly understood only because of the New Testament. These two together constitute the single Word of God. From the laws of Moses we learn to know Christ, and we learn how to direct our living in holiness and righteousness. The Ten Words of Horeb also possess continuing authority, even though we may understand that the shadows of the Torah are now for the most part fulfilled.

Q&A 93

Q. How are these commandments divided?

A. Into two parts. The first teaches us how to live in relation to God; the second, what duties we owe our neighbor.

When the LORD our God established a covenant with Israel at Sinai, he was clearly following a custom that had existed among the neighboring nations. Excavations from a later period have shown us this. It was customary to make two copies of the text of the treaty that the sovereign king made with his vassal, giving one copy to each party to place in the sanctuary of its god. God broke with that custom, however, for he gave Moses the mandate to place *both* tablets in the ark for preservation (Exod. 25:16). The word *table* refers to all Ten Commandments.

If God wrote the same things on both tablets, however, then we need look for no information in Holy Scripture in order to infer that we need to divide the Ten Commandments in a particular way. We can simply stick with the obvious order of our conduct first toward God and then toward our neighbor.

Q&A 94

Q. *What does the L*ORD *require in the first commandment?*

A. That for the sake of my very salvation I avoid and flee all idolatry, witchcraft, superstition, and prayer to saints or to other creatures. Further, that I rightly come to know the only true God, trust in him alone, submit to him with all humility and patience, expect all good from him only, and love, fear, and honor him with all my heart. In short, that I forsake all creatures rather than do the least thing against his will.

Q&A 95

Q. *What is idolatry?*

A. Idolatry is having or inventing something in which to put our trust instead of, or in addition to, the only true God who has revealed himself in his Word.

Nowhere in the book of Genesis, where the story of Israel in Egypt is narrated, do we read that Israel was involved with idols while living in Egypt, but in Joshua 24:14 and Ezekiel 20:8 we do read about that. The LORD knew very well that his people were not immune to this evil. He saw to it that the slaughter of sacrificial animals occurred only where he had commanded (Lev. 17:9; Deut. 12:14). Israel would be encountering idolatrous practices among her neighbors, who practiced such abominations as witchcraft, sorcery, spiritism, and the like. Scripture teaches that behind pagan idols lay the fearsome power of the demons (Lev. 17:7; Acts 26:18; Eph. 2:2; 1 Cor. 10:20). This reality lay behind the first commandment.

What the Lord forbids in the first commandment

Forgetting what they had heard about the LORD from their ancestors Adam and Noah, people began to invent their own objects of worship: the sun, moon, stars, rain, fertility, etc. No matter how influential these created beings are, Scripture calls them God's "servants" (Ps. 119:91).

The sin of idolatry can occur in two ways—when people worship and serve something else *instead of* the LORD, or when people worship and serve something else *alongside* the LORD. The former is found among pagan peoples and among those who have fallen away from the LORD, people who tend to make an idol out of Fate, or Being, or The Highest Essence. Idols can include the state, financial capital, the community—any thing or idea that replaces God in our affections and allegiance. The latter occurs when we have a divided heart, loving God and something or someone else as our deliverer. In Scripture this form of idolatry is often called whoredom, in comparison to the sin of a woman whose heart is divided with respect to her own husband.

In this commandment the LORD is also warning us against superstition, false ideas about God and creation that can imprison people and instill fear. Throughout Scripture and human history, people have turned to sources other than the LORD for their guidance, their well-being, and worship.

What the Lord requires in the first commandment

The Catechism properly summarizes Scripture's teaching about the opposite of idolatry, namely, the right knowledge of God. We cannot simply invent things about God, but must believe and say about him only what Scripture teaches. And we may consult his works to discover confirmation about God's character, and say with the psalmist, "The earth is full of the steadfast love of the LORD" (Ps. 33:5). Without rightly knowing God, we are unable to display his image in our godly righteousness and pure holiness (Col. 3:10).

In Scripture, to know God is to love God, as a husband and wife know and love each other (Exod. 2:25; 1 Sam. 2:12; 1 Chron. 28:9; Isa. 1:3; John 1:10; Rom. 8:29). This knowledge and love include *trust*. Such trust leads us to *submit* to God with humility and patience, especially in adversity. Our Savior demonstrated all of these features in his life on earth and was delivered by his heavenly Father from all his enemies, especially the enemy of death (Heb. 12:1–2).

In short, the first commandment requires that we love God with all our heart, that we fear making him angry by our sin, and that we respect him so much that we would forsake all other creatures rather than go against his will. That can include father, mother, and others who have authority over us (Matt. 10:37; Acts 5:29). The apostle John warns us, "The world is passing away along with its desires, but whoever does the will of God abides forever" (1 John 2:17).

Scripture References

Isaiah 45:22
> "Turn to me and be saved,
>   all the ends of the earth!
> For I am God, and there is no other."

Matthew 4:10
Then Jesus said to him, "Be gone, Satan! For it is written, 'You shall worship the Lord your God and him only shall you serve.'"

1 Chronicles 16:25–27
> For great is the LORD, and greatly to be praised,
>   and he is to be feared above all gods.
> For all the gods of the peoples are worthless idols,
>   but the LORD made the heavens.
> Splendor and majesty are before him;
>   strength and joy are in his place.

LORD'S DAY 35

Q&A 96

Q. *What does God require in the second commandment?*

A. We are not to make an image of God in any way, nor to worship him in any other manner than he has commanded in his Word.

Q&A 97

Q. *May we then not make any image at all?*

A. God cannot and may not be visibly portrayed in any way. Creatures may be portrayed, but God forbids us to make or have any images of them in order to worship them or to serve God through them.

Q&A 98

Q. *But may images not be tolerated in the churches as "books for the laity"?*

A. No, for we should not be wiser than God. He wants his people to be taught not by means of dumb images but by the living preaching of his Word.

In modern English we no longer use the word *jealous* with the same meaning as the Hebrew word *qannah* in Exodus 20:5. The Hebrew word for "jealousy" describes a husband whose wife has taken up with another man; such a man is filled with jealousy (Num. 5:14). It was not sufficient simply to honor Yahweh exclusively as God; Israel had to serve him in the proper way as well. Moses gave extensive instruction about that in Deuteronomy 4.

What God forbids in the second commandment

We may not make any image of God, even though making an image is impossible. No one has ever seen God (John 1:18; 1 Tim. 6:16). We are unable to make any image of God. Nevertheless, Aaron, Micah, and Jeroboam tried to do so. All of them made images of a bull, because a bull represented power and fertility. In doing so, they had in view the worship not of a strange god, but of Yahweh, who had delivered Israel from Egypt (Exod. 32:4–5). The same was true of king Jeroboam (1 Kings 12:28). He devoted his treasure to his self-directed service of God. But God called it a provocation (1 Kings 15:30). So God condemned also the self-directed legalism of the Pharisees (Gal. 1:8–9).

What God commands in the second commandment

The Lord Jesus told the Samaritan woman that true worshipers would worship the Father in spirit and in truth (John 4:23), which means in accordance with the teaching of the apostles. The Holy Spirit works within us with the written Bible and with the tangible sacraments.

To make or to desire to make an image of God is folly. But we certainly may portray and photograph people and objects.

Roman Catholics believe that they may use images in their church buildings as "books for the laity." The word *laity* is already unbiblical. We may not divide the church into clergy and laity (see the Pharisees, John 7:49).

Scripture References

Isaiah 40:18
> To whom then will you liken God,
>   or what likeness compare with him?

John 1:18

No one has ever seen God; the only God, who is at the Father's side, he has made him known.

1 Timothy 6:15–16

Which he will display at the proper time—he who is the blessed and only Sovereign, the King of kings and Lord of lords, who alone has immortality, who dwells in unapproachable light, whom no one has ever seen or can see. To him be honor and eternal dominion. Amen.

LORD'S DAY 36

In the first commandment God prohibited his church in the old dispensation from honoring any other god, and in the second commandment he prohibited them from serving him in a self-directed manner, for example, as the pagans worshiped their own invented gods in their own invented manner (that is, by means of "images"). Then follows the third commandment: you shall not take the name of Yahweh your God in vain, for Yahweh will not hold anyone guiltless who takes his name in vain.

Q&A 99

Q. *What is required in the third commandment?*

A. We are not to blaspheme or to abuse the name of God by cursing, perjury, or unnecessary oaths, nor to share in such horrible sins by being silent bystanders. Rather, we must use the holy name of God only with fear and reverence, so that we may rightly confess him, call upon him, and praise him in all our words and works.

Q&A 100

Q. *Is the blaspheming of God's name by swearing and cursing such a grievous sin that God is angry also with those who do not prevent and forbid it as much as they can?*

A. Certainly, for no sin is greater or provokes God's wrath more than the blaspheming of his name. That is why he commanded it to be punished with death.

Holy Scripture indicates that the Israelites were forbidden to take the names of idols on their lips (Exod. 23:13; Josh. 23:7; Ps. 16:4). But concerning God's name, Moses said, "You shall fear the LORD your God. You shall serve him and hold fast to him, and by his name you shall swear. He is your praise. He is your God" (Deut. 10:20–21). The composers of the psalms repeatedly praise the name of Yahweh, and the result is that the name of Yahweh was repeatedly praised in the singing of the people and the Levites.

God disclosed the deep meaning of that name most richly to Moses. At the burning bush, God foretold the salvation of his people from Egypt. God told Moses to tell the people, "Say this to the people of Israel, 'I AM has sent me to you.' ["I AM" means "I will surely be *with* you."] God also said to Moses, 'Say this to the people of Israel, 'The LORD, the God of your fathers, the God of Abraham, the God of Isaac, and the God of Jacob, has sent me to you.' This is my name forever, and thus I am to be remembered throughout all generations" (Exod. 3:14–15).

Shortly before Christ's birth Zachariah sang about God showing "the mercy promised to our fathers" and remembering "his holy covenant, the oath that he swore to our father Abraham" (Luke 1:72–73). Mary spoke the same way (Luke 1:54–55). For us the meaning of the name Yahweh is clear, namely, that God is the God *who makes alive*. He is the Helper and Deliverer. Therefore he has sent his beloved Son for the redemption not only of Israel but of the nations, of people who have not one drop of Abraham's blood in their veins (Luke 2:31–32; John 1:12; 3:16; Gal. 3:8, 26, 29; Eph. 2:12–13; 3:6; 1 John 2:2). The entire Bible is drawn together in the name Yahweh. This is why people must use the name of God reverently. It is the shortest summary of everything we know about God. It would be inconceivable for us to use the name of God or Father or Lord "in vain," that is, to use it senselessly, inconsiderately, mockingly. God commanded that such sinful abuse of his name must be punished with death (Lev. 24:16).

What God forbids in the third commandment

When Goliath mocked the name of Israel's God, that cost him his life. But it is of course equally terrible for someone to misuse God's name with reference to one's situation ("God damn it"). God also said, "You shall not swear by my name falsely, and so profane the name of your God: I am the LORD" (Lev. 19:12). The witnesses against Naboth were guilty of perjury (1 Kings 21:10, 13).

One must not swear a careless oath. The godly Joshua fell into that with the Gibeonites (Josh. 9). He kept his oath. God was very delighted by that.

The Lord Jesus disapproved of the Pharisees' swearing by the temple or by the gold of the temple (Matt. 23:16, 21–22).

God gets angry with us when we hear people using his name improperly and do nothing about it (Ps. 29:2).

What God commands in the third commandment

We must approach God respectfully, with deep reverence. In prosperity we must thank him, in adversity we must pray to him for help, at home and in the church speaking in psalms, hymns, and spiritual songs, singing and rejoicing to the honor of God (Eph. 5:19). We must be "a letter from Christ" (2 Cor. 3:3). If on occasion we use God's name in connection with swearing an oath, we must do so with reverence and must honor our oaths faithfully, even if that would be to our own loss (Pss. 15:4; 74:10; 139:20).

Scripture References

Exodus 3:15

God also said to Moses, "Say this to the people of Israel, 'The Lord, the God of your fathers, the God of Abraham, the God of Isaac, and the God of Jacob, has sent me to you.' This is my name forever, and thus I am to be remembered throughout all generations."

Deuteronomy 10:20–21

"You shall fear the Lord your God. You shall serve him and hold fast to him, and by his name you shall swear. He is your praise. He is your God, who has done for you these great and terrifying things that your eyes have seen."

Lord's Day 37

The time of the Reformation saw extensive discussion about oath swearing, so extensive that our forefathers devoted a separate Catechism Lord's Day in which they confessed God's Word in response to errors of the Anabaptists and the Roman Catholics.

Q&A 101

Q. *But may we swear an oath by the name of God in a godly manner?*

A. Yes, when the government demands it of its subjects, or when necessity requires it, in order to maintain and promote fidelity and truth, to God's glory and for our neighbor's good. Such oath-taking is based on God's Word and was therefore rightly used by saints in the Old and the New Testament.

Q&A 102

Q. *May we also swear by saints or other creatures?*

A. No. A lawful oath is a calling upon God, who alone knows the heart, to bear witness to the truth, and to punish me if I swear falsely. No creature is worthy of such honor.

The Anabaptists caused a lot of difficulty for their contemporaries. They claimed, for example, that princes "without understanding" (referring to Roman Catholics) did not need to be obeyed, which was incorrect. In addition, they thought it was improper to establish the word of godly people with an oath. For they were citizens of Zion, which had descended from heaven in Munster, Germany. Hence, it was no longer necessary to swear oaths.

To be sure, the Anabaptists appealed to the familiar words of the Lord Jesus, "Do not take an oath at all" (Matt. 5:34). But in saying this, the Savior was not forbidding every form of oath swearing. He himself testified under oath before his judge Caiaphas (Matt. 26:63–64).

The Roman Catholics went in the opposite direction. They swore oaths not only in the name of God, but also in the names of Mary, Peter, and other saints.

A proper oath formula is "As surely as God Almighty is my help."

To swear an oath is to call on God as witness that one is speaking the truth (in connection with a declaratory oath) or that one's intention is upright (in the case of a promissory oath). God knows, for he is omniscient (Ps. 139).

Scripture Reference

Deuteronomy 6:13
"It is the LORD your God you shall fear. Him you shall serve and by his name you shall swear."

LORD'S DAY 38

Q&A 103

Q. *What does God require in the fourth commandment?*

A. First, that the ministry of the gospel and the schools be maintained and that, especially on the day of rest, I diligently attend the church of God to hear God's Word, to use the sacraments, to call publicly upon the LORD, and to give Christian offerings for the poor. Second, that all the days of my life I rest from my evil works, let the LORD work in me through his Holy Spirit, and so begin in this life the eternal Sabbath.

The fourth commandment reads this way: "Remember the Sabbath day, to keep it holy. Six days you shall labor, and do all your work, but the seventh day is a Sabbath to the LORD your God. On it you shall not do any work, you, or your son, or your daughter, your male servant, or your female servant, or your livestock, or the sojourner who is within your gates. For in six days the LORD made heaven and earth, the sea, and all that is in them, and rested on the seventh day. Therefore the LORD blessed the Sabbath day and made it holy" (Exod. 20:8–11).

To *remember* is the same as what we read in Deuteronomy 5:12: "*Observe* the Sabbath day, to keep it holy." That is to say, separate this day unto the service of Yahweh. On that day Israel was to forgo all work, even during the seasons of plowing and harvesting. How strange that must have seemed later to the Gentiles in Canaan! What a different nation Israel is, they would have thought. Indeed, that was the case. God himself called that day a sign of the covenant that he had made with Israel (Exod. 31:13, 16–17). Israel had been delivered out of the house of slavery in Egypt and needed now to work only for their food and drink, though not on the Sabbath day itself. On that day everyone was permitted to rest, to participate in the assemblies to which they were called by the sound of silver trumpets blown by the priests (Lev. 19:3; 23:3; Num. 10:8). At that time Sabbath sacrifices were to be brought into God's presence, namely, twice as many as were brought each day throughout the week (Num. 28:9).

Unfortunately Israel was far from faithful in keeping this commandment. In conflict with God's commandment (Lev. 25:2–3), Israel farmed the land during the sabbatical years. Therefore God allowed the land to enjoy all those missed rest periods when he sent Israel away into captivity (2 Chron. 36:21).

When the Lord Jesus was on earth, the Pharisees oppressed Israel by turning that beautiful day into something torturous, because everything was forbidden on the Sabbath. For example, people were not allowed to walk beyond a Sabbath's journey, which was no farther than what one could walk in a quarter hour.

Our Savior obeyed the fourth commandment. It was his custom to go each Sabbath to the synagogue (Luke 4:16). But he refused to honor the self-invented rules of the scribes. He preferred to heal the sick precisely on the Sabbath (Mark 3:1–5). He said, "The Sabbath was made for man, not man for the Sabbath" (Mark 2:27). On the Sabbath even slaves were supposed to rest, and even the animals were supposed to catch their breath (Deut. 5:14). As children of their heavenly Father, the Israelites were allowed to follow his example and rest from their work. When Jesus traveled through Galilee on the Sabbath and preached in the synagogues and performed healings, he never disapproved of his disciples when they plucked grain, ground it in their hand, and ate it. To the complaint of the Pharisees he responded that the Son of Man was Lord also of the Sabbath (Mark 2:28).

In the rest of the New Testament we read that the Lord Jesus fulfilled the Sabbath more gloriously than anyone before him, for by his suffering and death he put an end to the celebration of the Sabbath of the Old Testament (Gal. 4:10; Col. 2:16–17). The

Sabbath was the sign of the Horeb covenant (Exod. 31:17) that the LORD had established with Israel. Now that this covenant is antiquated and has disappeared (Heb. 8:13), the Sabbath is also antiquated and has disappeared along with it. One who considers all days to be alike is not condemned by the apostle Paul (Rom. 14:5; Col. 2:16).

Scripture Reference

Colossians 2:16–17

Therefore let no one pass judgment on you in questions of food and drink, or with regard to a festival or a new moon or a Sabbath. These are a shadow of the things to come, but the substance belongs to Christ.

LORD'S DAY 39

The fifth commandment reads this way: "Honor your father and your mother, that your days may be long in the land that the LORD your God is giving you" (Exod. 20:12).

In this connection the Catechism confesses the following.

Q&A 104

Q. *What does God require in the fifth commandment?*

A. That I show all honor, love, and faithfulness to my father and mother and to all those in authority over me, submit myself with due obedience to their good instruction and discipline, and also have patience with their weaknesses and shortcomings, since it is God's will to govern us by their hand.

The fifth commandment is the commandment dealing with authority. The word *honor* here does not mean the same as love, for that cannot be practiced toward all parents. But the *honor* being spoken of in the fifth commandment means "acknowledge as weighty."

From the rest of Scripture we learn that we must honor not just our father and mother, but all who have been placed over us. Sometimes the term *father* is used with reference to a teacher (2 Kgs. 2:12), and judges and rulers are called "gods" (Pss. 82:1, 6; 138:1). The Lord Jesus told Pilate the governor, "You would have no authority over me at all unless it had been given you from above" (John 19:11). The apostle Paul wrote, "Let every person be subject to the governing authorities. For there is no authority except from God, and those that exist have been instituted by God" (Rom. 13:1). So the Catechism states correctly that we must obey all who have been appointed to be over us, "since it is God's will to govern us by their hand."

That authority, however, is not without limits. A father may not give his son a sinful command. Joseph was not disobeying God when he refused to obey Potiphar's wife, who had commanded him to commit adultery with her. The apostles received from the Sanhedrin a command to be silent about Jesus, but they responded by saying that they needed to decide whether it was right in God's sight to obey man rather than God (Acts 5:29). The government in turn is also a servant of God (Rom. 13:4).

The fifth commandment must be obeyed first within the family. Children of Christian parents are baptized and thus must live according to God's covenant. Those parents nurture their children in the teaching and admonition of the Lord (Eph. 6:4). At the baptism of each child the church prays that God would rule this child with his Holy Spirit, so that this child would be reared in a Christian and God-fearing manner.

As the children grow, teachers in school must remember that these children have been entrusted to them, children upon whom the Owner's mark of the Lord Jesus has been placed by means of baptism. Timothy was instructed in the Holy Scripture by his grandmother Lois and mother Eunice (2 Tim. 1:5; 3:15).

If occasionally as children we are treated unfairly by our parents, then we should follow the example of patience that our Savior has given in such situations (1 Pet. 2:21, 23). If matters go from bad to worse, then we must appeal to our grandparents or to our ecclesiastical leaders or to our civil government. But we must repay especially the good that our parents have done for us. Just before his death our Savior provided another son to his mother, namely, John, who from that moment on took her into his home (John 19:25–27).

Although it is God who has clothed the church's office-bearers with authority, they must not abuse this authority. Notice how the Christian church has grown into a worldly state with rulers (cardinals) and an "infallible pope" as head. No, then we must

hear the apostle Peter in 1 Peter 5:1–3, where he calls himself simply "a fellow elder" together with the other elders.

We ought also to honor the civil governments. Let us pray
faithfully for them in our gatherings and in our family prayers.
But governments can also have evildoers among them. Our Savior spoke of Herod, the murderer of John the Baptist, as "that
fox" (Luke 13:32).

The good rule remains: Fear God, honor the king (1 Pet.
2:13, 17).

Scripture References

Luke 2:51–52
And he went down with them and came to Nazareth and was submissive
to them. And his mother treasured up all these things in her heart. And
Jesus increased in wisdom and in stature and in favor with God and man.

Acts 5:29
But Peter and the apostles answered, "We must obey God rather
than men."

LORD'S DAY 40

Q&A 105

Q. *What does God require in the sixth commandment?*

A. I am not to dishonor, hate, injure, or kill my neighbor by thoughts, words, or gestures, and much less by deeds, whether personally or through another; rather, I am to put away all desire of revenge. Moreover, I am not to harm or recklessly endanger myself. Therefore, also, the government bears the sword to prevent murder.

Q&A 106

Q. *But does this commandment speak only of killing?*

A. By forbidding murder God teaches us that he hates the root of murder, such as envy, hatred, anger, and desire of revenge, and that he regards all these as murder.

Q&A 107

Q. *Is it enough, then, that we do not kill our neighbor in any such way?*

A. No. When God condemns envy, hatred, and anger, he commands us to love our neighbor as ourselves, to show patience, peace, gentleness, mercy, and friendliness toward him, to protect him from harm as much as we can, and to do good even to our enemies.

If there is one sin that appeared upon earth quickly and frequently, it was murder. Men like Cain and Lamech make us tremble. Despite the severe punishment of the flood, God thought it necessary to issue this command: "Whoever sheds the blood of man, by man shall his blood be shed, for God made man in his own image" (Gen. 9:6).

The sixth commandment was far from superfluous for Israel, the Old Testament church. Recall Saul (against David) or Ahab (against Naboth). The Lord Jesus pointed to the long trail of blood resulting from the killing of the prophets in Israel (Luke 11:50–51). He himself was killed by church people, although Pilate and his wife tried to rescue him (Acts 2:23; 4:10), whereas at that time and in later periods the sad phenomenon appeared of the church committing murder against the church, something that shames us and removes any reason for us to look down on anyone else, no matter who they might be. Church people are by nature still sinful people, something evident from their mutual fighting, which happens repeatedly and continuously.

When our Savior was on earth, the opinion prevailed among the Jews that everything was fine as long as one never killed another person, committed adultery, stole from anybody, or the like. At any rate, that is how the Pharisees thought, as well as the rich young man (Matt. 19:20; Luke 18:11). But the Lord Jesus said, "But I say to you that everyone who is angry with his brother will be liable to judgment; whoever insults his brother will be liable to the council; and whoever says, 'You fool!' will be liable to the hell of fire" (Matt. 5:22). Indeed, Scripture is full of warnings against an angry heart (Gen. 4:6 [Cain]; 1 John 3:12): "You shall not hate your brother in your heart" (Lev. 19:17).

Nor is it sufficient simply if we do not hate our neighbor. Jesus said, "You shall love your neighbor as yourself" (Matt. 22:39; Mark 12:31; see Luke 10:27). Only then is the sixth commandment being fulfilled. Indeed, the law did contain the provision of "eye for eye, tooth for tooth," but that regulation was given to the government (Deut. 19:16–21). The Savior said, "But I say to you, 'Do not resist the one who is evil. But if anyone slaps you on the right cheek [a genuinely Jewish insult, done with the back of the hand], turn to him the other also'" (Matt. 5:39). He added, "Love your enemies and pray for those who persecute you, so that you may be sons of your Father who is in heaven. For he makes his sun rise on the evil and on the good, and sends rain on the just and on the unjust" (Matt. 5:44–45).

Consider God's goodness toward the animals of Nineveh. Consider the generous conduct of the prophet Elisha toward captives (2 Kgs. 6:15–23).

The Lord Jesus was entirely correct in saying, "So whatever you wish that others would do to you, do also to them, for this is the [fulfillment of the] Law and the Prophets" (Matt. 7:12).

Subsequently the apostles preached, "If your enemy is hungry, feed him; if he is thirsty, give him something to drink; for by so doing you will heap burning coals on his head" (Rom. 12:20, citing from Prov. 25:21–22).

Naturally we cannot love everyone in the same manner that children love their parents or spouses love each other. Loving our neighbor means seeking what is good for him, treating him and his property just as well as we treat ourselves and our own property (Exod. 23:5).

Scripture References

Exodus 23:5
"If you see the donkey of one who hates you lying down under its burden, you shall refrain from leaving him with it; you shall rescue it with him."

Leviticus 19:17–18
"You shall not hate your brother in your heart, but you shall reason frankly with your neighbor, lest you incur sin because of him. You shall not take vengeance or bear a grudge against the sons of your own people, but you shall love your neighbor as yourself: I am the Lord."

LORD'S DAY 41

Marriage was instituted by God himself, before sin entered the world, when God gave Adam a mutual helper suited to him. Both were of the same flesh. The beautiful story about this in Genesis 2:18–25 concludes with the instruction that the husband must leave his father and mother and hold fast to his wife, and they shall be one flesh (Gen. 2:24).

That a man and a woman who are married to each other constitute a unity that may not be arbitrarily broken was taught by the Lord Jesus this way: "What therefore God has joined together, let not man separate" (Matt. 19:6). The apostle Paul commands that each man must "control his own body in holiness and honor," not in passionate desire, like the pagans (1 Thess. 4:4–5). A marriage need not obtain a formal blessing at all, although we may certainly ask God for a blessing on our marriages. But that ceremony is not needed because at its origin marriage was not something immoral. For then the Lord Jesus would not have attended the wedding at Cana (John 2), and Paul would not have compared the relationship between husband and wife to the relationship between Christ and his church (Eph. 5:23–25).

Unfortunately, the first human sin that defiled everything affected marriage as well. Lamech took for himself two wives (Gen. 4:19), and men of nobility took even more wives (Gen. 6:1–2). Women were often given away as gifts, or they were sold or kidnapped. That was the fulfillment of God's warning that he had given to Eve: ". . . and he shall rule over you" (Gen. 3:16). This warning remains valid in our day.

The seventh commandment is formulated in Hebrew with the masculine form of the verb. But just as with the other commandments, here as well the feminine form must be seen as included. For example, God commanded not only that the adulterer was to be put to death, but the adulteress as well (Lev. 20:10; Deut. 22:21–22).

All forms of unchastity and impurity have been forbidden from ancient times. These sins were very prevalent among the nations surrounding Israel. In Egypt brothers and sisters married, fathers and daughters as well. Among the Canaanites there was sodomy, something that was threatened against the angels who were visiting Lot (Gen. 19:5). This sin was committed especially among pagans in their idol temples. Centuries later, Paul writes that in his day shameful acts were committed by men with men and by women with women (Rom. 1:26–27). In the seventh commandment God mentioned only one sin, but from the broad discussion given by Moses in Deuteronomy 22:12–23:14, it is evident how large a number of transgressions are covered by this commandment.

Christians are the property of Christ, so they must conduct themselves according to that exalted position when it comes to marriage. This explains the Catechism's admirable confession.

Q&A 108

Q. *What does the seventh commandment teach us?*

A. That all unchastity is cursed by God. We must therefore detest it from the heart and live chaste and disciplined lives, both within and outside of holy marriage.

Q&A 109

Q. *Does God in this commandment forbid nothing more than adultery and similar shameful sins?*

A. Since we, body and soul, are temples of the Holy Spirit, it is God's will that we keep ourselves pure and holy. Therefore he forbids all unchaste acts, gestures, words, thoughts, desires, and whatever may entice us to unchastity.

God forbids not only impure acts but also impure words, indeed, even impure thoughts. The Lord Jesus said, "Everyone who looks at a woman with lustful intent has already committed adultery with her in his heart" (Matt. 5:28). The apostles later pointed in the same direction: "But sexual immorality and all impurity or covetousness must not even be named among you, as is proper among saints" (Eph. 5:3). Such people will not inherit the kingdom of Christ and of God (Eph. 5:5). Evil company corrupts good morals (1 Cor. 15:33). Our body is not for sexual immorality but for the Lord Jesus, for it belongs to him. God not only raised the Lord Jesus Christ, but through his power he will raise us as well: "Do you not know that your bodies are members of Christ? . . . Or do you not know that your body is a temple of the Holy Spirit within you, whom you have from God? You are not your own, for you were bought with a price. So glorify God in your body" (1 Cor. 6:15, 19–20).

Children must not read any shameful books and must not dress carelessly. They must protect themselves from unnatural sins, such as those committed by men with each other and women with each other. Temptation can begin very early. Even within marriage, we must not live in terms of our own appetites. Jesus placed his hand upon us when we were born as covenant children, and therefore baptized. And so young people must keep God's covenant in mind when they look for a husband or wife. Don't go after an unbeliever (2 Cor. 6:14–15). Don't forget that the Lord Jesus has placed his claim upon you and your ancestors perhaps for centuries already.

Husbands, seek your happiness with your own wife and not

with the wife of another: "Drink water from your own cistern, flowing water from your own well" (Prov. 5:15); "Husbands, live with your wives in an understanding way, showing honor to the woman as the weaker vessel, since they are heirs with you of the grace of life, so that your prayers may not be hindered" (1 Pet. 3:7).

Scripture References

Matthew 19:4–6
He answered, "Have you not read that he who created them from the beginning made them male and female, and said, 'Therefore a man shall leave his father and his mother and hold fast to his wife, and the two shall become one flesh'? So they are no longer two but one flesh. What therefore God has joined together, let not man separate."

1 Corinthians 6:13
"Food is meant for the stomach and the stomach for food"—and God will destroy both one and the other. The body is not meant for sexual immorality, but for the Lord, and the Lord for the body.

1 Peter 3:3–4
Do not let your adorning be external—the braiding of hair and the putting on of gold jewelry, or the clothing you wear—but let your adorning be the hidden person of the heart with the imperishable beauty of a gentle and quiet spirit, which in God's sight is very precious.

LORD'S DAY 42

Stealing can occur in such a way that only one person is duped, or such that an entire people is robbed. You need only look at how Israel was persecuted in Egypt. When God came with his punishments (the plagues), the Egyptians urgently pleaded that the Israelites leave their land. At their departure, the Egyptians loaded the Israelites down with treasures like gold and silver. People must properly understand the metaphor that we read in Exodus 3:22, where it says that at her departure, Israel plundered Egypt. The fact that God acted according to his timetable was evident also with Israel's exodus. And before Israel entered the land of Canaan, Moses said, "And what great nation is there, that has statutes and rules so righteous as all this law that I set before you today?" (Deut. 4:8). At that point Moses gave wide-ranging instruction about each commandment.

Sadly, the eighth commandment was subsequently transgressed all too often in Israel's own land. And this, even though God had so clearly warned them through Moses. If Israel transgressed the eighth commandment, God would punish them: "And the heavens over your head shall be bronze, and the earth under you shall be iron" (Deut. 28:23). Following such pleasant times as those of David, for example, when each sat under his vine and fig tree, the Israelites were at other times parched by a drought lasting a couple of years. During Ahab's time the heavens became bronze.

See how the prophets had to warn against transgressing God's law, including the eighth commandment (Isa. 5:8; Mic. 2:2). Nevertheless, the punishment of captivity came upon Israel.

When the Lord Jesus came to earth, he encountered teachers of the law who gave the appearance of being very pious but "who devour[ed] widows' houses" (Mark 12:40). But the Lord Jesus commanded, "Love your enemies, and do good, and lend, expecting nothing in return" (Luke 6:35). The apostles, like James, for example, spoke in the same manner, and Paul wrote, "I coveted no one's silver or gold or apparel. . . . [R]emember the words of the Lord Jesus, how he himself said, 'It is more blessed to give than to receive'" (Acts 20:33, 35).

Q&A 110

Q. *What does God forbid in the eighth commandment?*

A. God forbids not only outright theft and robbery but also such wicked schemes and devices as false weights and measures, deceptive merchandising, counterfeit money, and usury; we must not defraud our neighbor in any way, whether by force or by show of right. In addition God forbids all greed and all abuse or squandering of his gifts.

Q&A 111

Q. *What does God require of you in this commandment?*

A. I must promote my neighbor's good wherever I can and may, deal with him as I would like others to deal with me, and work faithfully so that I may be able to give to those in need.

In connection with the eighth commandment, we can see how wide a difference exists between the first and the second part of our conversion or regeneration. One of two things must be true: either we transgress the commandment, "You shall not steal," or we observe it.

The former, transgressing this commandment, occurs when we appropriate or want to appropriate for ourselves something that belongs to another, as if money and property were the supreme power. God doesn't give any part of this world into our possession in order that we might flaunt it or live excessively from it, but in order that we might use it with a thankful heart, whether eating or drinking, whether clothing or dwelling. We should be so sympathetic toward others with what God has entrusted to us that that our own sandwich would taste terrible as long as our neighbor is suffering hunger: "But if anyone has the world's goods and sees his brother in need, yet closes his heart against him, how does God's love abide in him?" (1 John 3:17); "Come now, you rich, weep and howl for the miseries that are coming upon you. Your riches have rotted and your garments are moth-eaten. Your gold and silver have corroded, and their corrosion will be evidence against you and will eat your flesh like fire. You have laid up treasure in the last days. Behold, the wages of the laborers who mowed your fields, which you kept back by fraud, are crying out against you, and the cries of the harvesters have reached the ears of the Lord of hosts. You have lived on the earth in luxury and in self-indulgence. You have fattened your hearts in a day of slaughter" (Jas. 5:1–5).

Pickpockets and burglars are not the only thieves.

So here is the second part. We have already recalled the saying of Jesus, "It is more blessed to give than to receive" (Acts 20:35). He is also thought to have said once, "Whatever you do not want to be done to you, that you must not do against another." At least, that's how we repeat the adage. But the Lord Jesus actually said, "So whatever you wish that others would do to you, do also to them, for this is the Law and the Prophets" (Matt. 7:12). The matter was stated far more positively, for it declares what we must do. Moreover, people living in Jesus's day knew the ancient commandment "You shall love your neighbor as yourself" (Lev. 19:18; Matt. 22:39).

Nowhere in Scripture is honest business forbidden. In the Middle Ages charging interest on capital that had been loaned was often viewed as impermissible. But the Lord Jesus never disapproved of ordinary business. It is indeed wrong to take advantage of another person's need by demanding excessive interest. That is usury. The Lord Jesus did not speak at all disapprovingly about honest banking (Luke 19:23). The eighth commandment requires us to observe it temperately. Work with zeal, live in such a way that you have something left for needy people: "So then, as we have opportunity, let us do good to everyone, and especially to those who are of the household of faith" (Gal. 6:10).

Scripture Reference

Luke 16:1–9

He also said to the disciples, "There was a rich man who had a manager, and charges were brought to him that this man was wasting his possessions. And he called him and said to him, 'What is this that I hear about you? Turn in the account of your management, for you can no longer be manager.' And the manager said to himself, 'What shall I do, since my master is taking the management away from me? I am not strong enough to dig, and I am ashamed to beg. I have decided what to do, so that when I am removed from management, people may receive me into their houses.' So, summoning his master's debtors one by one, he said to the first, 'How much do you owe my master?' He said, 'A hundred measures of oil.' He said to him, 'Take your bill, and sit down quickly and write fifty.' Then he said to another, 'And how much do you owe?' He said, 'A hundred measures of wheat.' He said to him, 'Take your bill, and write eighty.' The master commended the dishonest manager for his shrewdness. For the sons of this world are more shrewd in dealing with their own generation than the sons of light. And I tell you, make friends for yourselves by means of unrighteous wealth, so that when it fails they may receive you into the eternal dwellings."

LORD'S DAY 43

Lying occurred in Paradise already, with the serpent, who said to Eve, "Did God actually say, 'You shall not eat of any tree in the garden'?" (Gen. 3:1). At that point Eve stated that Adam and she were permitted to eat of every tree except from the tree that stood in the middle of the garden. But when the serpent argued that she would not die, that was an absolute lie. This lie came from Satan, as the Lord Jesus taught when he said to some Jews who were opposing the truth: "You are of your father the devil, and your will is to do your father's desires. He was a murderer from the beginning, and does not stand in the truth, because there is no truth in him. When he lies, he speaks out of his own character, for he is a liar and the father of lies" (John 8:44). Therefore our heavenly Father gave the ninth commandment to his people after saving them from Egypt: "You shall not bear false testimony against your neighbor." With these words God's people were forbidden to lie before the judge. Translated literally, the ninth commandment reads this way, "You shall not answer against your neighbor as a witness of the lie." The Catechism expands upon this as follows.

Q&A 112

Q. *What is required in the ninth commandment?*

A. I must not give false testimony against anyone, twist no one's words, not gossip or slander, nor condemn or join in condemning anyone rashly and unheard. Rather, I must avoid all lying and deceit as the devil's own works, under penalty of God's heavy wrath. In court and everywhere else, I must love the truth, speak and confess it honestly, and do what I can to defend and promote my neighbor's honor and reputation.

Let us consider once again what is here forbidden and commanded.

What God forbids us in the ninth commandment

Lying before a judge usually happens under oath and is very disturbing to read about. Think about the stories involving Naboth, or the Lord Jesus, or Stephen. In daily life as well, lying is a serious sin and not simply a mistake, since it involves intentional falsehood or practicing pretense. David complained about this (Pss. 41; 52; 55). The Lord Jesus had a betrayer among his disciples. James writes, "The tongue is a fire, a world of unrighteousness. . . . It is a restless evil, full of deadly poison" (James 3:6, 8).

A Christian must guard against backbiting and slander, though these two words do not mean the same thing. *Backbiting* involves speaking evil unnecessarily about one's neighbor, even if what is said is true. But if it is unnecessary, then one is sinning against the command that it is better to cover the iniquity of one's neighbor. But *slander* involves intentionally speaking falsehood with evil intention to cause someone harm.

The Lord Jesus warned, "Judge not [that is, without basis] that you be not judged [on the last day]" (Matt. 7:1). For God will perform justice for the oppressed (Ps. 146:7). Paul warned about a time when God would send a strong delusion, "so that they may believe what is false" (2 Thess. 2:10–11).

What God commands us in the ninth commandment

After the return of the exiles from Babylon, the heart of the remnant was far from excited. The rebuilding of the city and the temple did not proceed very well. People suffered trouble from without (Samaritans) and from within. God provided comfort to the remnant through the prophet Zechariah by reminding them not to assume that God was still angry with them. He would cause a blessed future to dawn for Jerusalem. Old men and old women would sit in the city square, and the city would be full of boys and girls playing in its streets. What must they do? Hold days of fasting? No, these are the things they must do: "Speak the truth to one another; render in your gates judgments that are true [justice was declared in the square behind the gate] and make for peace; do not devise evil in your hearts against one another, and love no false oath, for all these things I hate, declares the LORD. . . . Therefore love truth and peace" (Zech. 8:16–17, 19). When the truth must be spoken, then let it be spoken especially in and by the court. This commandment applies to all of life. In connection with business, for example, we must keep our word even if it hurts us to do so (Ps. 15:4). Jesus commanded, "Let what you say be simply 'Yes' or 'No'" (Matt. 5:37). In the Greek world lying was not condemned per se, but only if one had not lied cleverly enough and was discovered. Paul wrote, "Therefore, having put away falsehood, let each one of you speak the truth with his neighbor, for we are members one of another" (Eph. 4:25); "Do not lie to one another, seeing that you have put off the old self with its practices and have put on the new self, which is being renewed in knowledge after the image of its creator" (Col. 3:9–10). No one is obligated always to say all that he knows, but whatever we do say must be true. David was so concerned that he might say something untrue about God's leading of him, that he said, "Set a guard, O LORD, over my mouth; keep watch over the door of my lips!" (Ps. 141:3). When people pursue theology, they must ensure that in speaking about God, they do not say things that are not in Holy Scripture, for then they cannot pray, "Hallowed be thy name."

We must also guard against giving our neighbor a bad name. The phrase "do what I can" means doing what one can to defend one's neighbor. A good name is a glorious inheritance that we give our descendants. If necessary, we must stand up for the good name of our neighbor. That is what Jonathan did against his father Saul, for example, on behalf of David (1 Sam. 19). The Lord Jesus commanded, "Whatever you wish that others would do to you, do also to them, for this is the Law and the Prophets" (Matt. 7:12).

Scripture References

Genesis 3:1-6
Now the serpent was more crafty than any other beast of the field that the LORD God had made.

He said to the woman, "Did God actually say, 'You shall not eat of any tree in the garden'?" And the woman said to the serpent, "We may eat of the fruit of the trees in the garden, but God said, 'You shall not eat of the fruit of the tree that is in the midst of the garden, neither shall you touch it, lest you die.'" But the serpent said to the woman, "You will not surely die. For God knows that when you eat of it your eyes will be opened, and you will be like God, knowing good and evil." So when the woman saw that the tree was good for food, and that it was a delight to the eyes, and that the tree was to be desired to make one wise, she took of its fruit and ate, and she also gave some to her husband who was with her, and he ate.

John 8:44
"You are of your father the devil, and your will is to do your father's desires. He was a murderer from the beginning, and does not stand in the truth, because there is no truth in him. When he lies, he speaks out of his own character, for he is a liar and the father of lies."

2 Thessalonians 2:11
Therefore God sends them a strong delusion, so that they may believe what is false.

Revelation 20:2
And he seized the dragon, that ancient serpent, who is the devil and Satan, and bound him for a thousand years.

LORD'S DAY 44

Q&A 113

Q. *What does the tenth commandment require of us?*

A. That not even the slightest thought or desire contrary to any of God's commandments should ever arise in our heart. Rather, with all our heart we should always hate all sin and delight in all righteousness.

Every observant Bible reader knows that the Ten Commandments appear twice in Scripture, first in Exodus 20 and later in Deuteronomy 5, the book of Moses par excellence. Following the Ten Commandments, Moses included an extensive discussion of each of them except the tenth commandment. Were we to ask Moses how that happened, supposing we could, he would respond to us with the counter question whether we had noticed that with all the preceding commandments he had already included the tenth. He had been discussing our heart with respect to all the other commandments.

This is an unforgettable lesson. A sinful desire in your heart precedes a sinful action. So consider that beforehand. This is what the Catechism is teaching us here.

What God forbids us in the tenth commandment

There are both good and bad desires. Formerly the Ephesians had walked according to the desires of the flesh, wrote the apostle, doing the will of the body and of the mind (Eph. 2:3). The same apostle wrote to Timothy, "Flee youthful passions" (2 Tim. 2:22). The Lord Jesus warned us not to allow the Word of God to be choked like seed sown among thistles: "But the cares of the world and the deceitfulness of riches and the desires for other things enter in and choke the word, and it proves unfruitful" (Mark 4:19). Therefore we must pray, "Who can discern his errors? Declare me innocent from hidden faults" (Ps. 19:12).

What God commands us in the tenth commandment

When David had sinned very wickedly, he confessed not only his sins when he prayed, "Against you, you only, have I sinned" (Ps. 51:4) but he confessed his sinful nature with which he was born, and he pleaded, "Create in me a clean heart, O God, and renew a right spirit within me" (Ps. 51:10). Paul commanded, "Walk by the Spirit, and you will not gratify the desires of the flesh" (Gal. 5:16). When our heart has become a dwelling place for Christ and his Spirit, his enemies become our enemies and everything that he commands us becomes our preferred desire.

Q&A 114

Q. *But can those converted to God keep these commandments perfectly?*

A. No. In this life even the holiest have only a small beginning of this obedience. Nevertheless, with earnest purpose they do begin to live not only according to some but to all the commandments of God.

Scripture teaches us definitely not to claim that believers keep God's commandments perfectly. It does tell us about Noah and his drunkenness (Gen. 9:21); Abraham, who submitted to Sarai's pressure that he take Hagar as a concubine and conceive the promised seed with her (Gen. 16:2); Isaac and Jacob, who lied (Gen. 26:7; 27:19); Lot, who chose to live in Sodom; and we read similar things about Moses, David, and others. Therefore Psalm 143:2 says, "Enter not into judgment with your servant, for no one living is righteous before you."

Nevertheless, we must not claim that no good thing dwelt within these believers. They were sinners "by nature" (see Q&A 5), but we read that Noah built the ark as a continuous and extended labor of faith. And recall how many good things are said about David! When Hezekiah learned he was about to die, he prayed, "Now, O Lord, please remember how I have walked before you in faithfulness and with a whole heart, and have done what is good in your sight" (2 Kgs. 20:3). Today as well, believers may sing with an honest heart psalms like Psalm 19 and Psalm 119.

Q&A 115

Q. *If in this life no one can keep the Ten Commandments perfectly, why does God have them preached so strictly?*

A. First, so that throughout our life we may more and more become aware of our sinful nature, and therefore seek more eagerly the forgiveness of sins and righteousness in Christ. Second, so that, while praying to God for the grace of the Holy Spirit, we may never stop striving to be renewed more and more after God's image, until after this life we reach the goal of perfection.

In Holy Scripture God continually holds before us his commandments. For example, when the apostle commands the Ephesians and Colossians to put to death the old nature and to put on the new nature, that is a command of the Spirit to keep all of God's commandments. Unfortunately, all of us fall short. By means of the preaching of God's Word, however, we discern our sinfulness and our sinful thoughts, words, and deeds, and we feel ourselves driven more and more to seek refuge in our Lord Jesus Christ, for his blood and Spirit. We need the first, his blood, for the forgiveness of sins, and the second, his Spirit, to forsake our sins more and more.

No one who sees himself in the mirror of God's commandments can say he lacks nothing. On the contrary, when Paul saw his continual sinning and deficiencies in the light of God's law, he considered himself to be a wretched man (Rom. 7:24). But faithful preaching of God's commandments is not designed to make us despair. On the contrary, it drives us to make faithful use of Jesus's blood, which we know supplies us with our *justification*. And this is the second thing that is closely connected with it. We may confess our sins, with the promised result. But then we must also want to forsake them. Therefore we must pray for a share not only in Christ's blood but also in Christ's Spirit. Well then, anyone who is being led by the Spirit of Christ is more and more renewed in the image of God, and delights to live in righteousness and holiness. That is the second fruit of our faith, namely, our regeneration. So the preaching of the Ten Commandments does not drive us to despair. But it does compel us to conclude our prayer with the petition that henceforth our old nature may diminish, and that we may live a godly life before the eyes of God and others.

Scripture References

Mark 7:1–23

Now when the Pharisees gathered to him, with some of the scribes who had come from Jerusalem, they saw that some of his disciples ate with hands that were defiled, that is, unwashed. (For the Pharisees and all the Jews do not eat unless they wash their hands properly, holding to the tradition of the elders, and when they come from the marketplace, they do not eat unless they wash. And there are many other traditions that they observe, such as the washing of cups and pots and copper vessels and dining couches.) And the Pharisees and the scribes asked him, "Why do your disciples not walk according to the tradition of the elders, but eat with defiled hands?" And he said to them, "Well did Isaiah prophesy of you hypocrites, as it is written,

> "'This people honors me with their lips,
>   but their heart is far from me;
> in vain do they worship me,
>   teaching as doctrines the commandments of men.'

"You leave the commandment of God and hold to the tradition of men."
    And he said to them, "You have a fine way of rejecting the commandment of God in order to establish your tradition! For Moses said, 'Honor

your father and your mother'; and, 'Whoever reviles father or mother must surely die.' But you say, 'If a man tells his father or his mother, "Whatever you would have gained from me is Corban"' (that is, given to God)—then you no longer permit him to do anything for his father or mother, thus making void the word of God by your tradition that you have handed down. And many such things you do."

And he called the people to him again and said to them, "Hear me, all of you, and understand: There is nothing outside a person that by going into him can defile him, but the things that come out of a person are what defile him." And when he had entered the house and left the people, his disciples asked him about the parable. And he said to them, "Then are you also without understanding? Do you not see that whatever goes into a person from outside cannot defile him, since it enters not his heart but his stomach, and is expelled?" (Thus he declared all foods clean.) And he said, "What comes out of a person is what defiles him. For from within, out of the heart of man, come evil thoughts, sexual immorality, theft, murder, adultery, coveting, wickedness, deceit, sensuality, envy, slander, pride, foolishness. All these evil things come from within, and they defile a person."

Romans 7:7
What then shall we say? That the law is sin? By no means! Yet if it had not been for the law, I would not have known sin. For I would not have known what it is to covet if the law had not said, "You shall not covet."

LORD'S DAY 45

> ## Q&A 116
>
> **Q.** *Why is prayer necessary for Christians?*
>
> **A.** Because prayer is the most important part of the thankfulness that God requires of us. Moreover, God will give his grace and the Holy Spirit only to those who constantly and with heartfelt longing ask him for these gifts and thank him for them.

What Christian would retire to bed in the evening without having thanked his heavenly Father for the day that the Father has added to his life? For we owe our life to God. He is our Creator, and furthermore, he has made us his children by allowing the gospel to be brought to our ancestors, so that many of us have been born as members of God's covenant people. We must thank God daily for that, and do so honestly and uprightly. We must begin with acknowledging and worshiping God reverently as our Father.

The question arises at this point: What is a proper prayer?

Q&A 117

Q. *What belongs to a prayer that pleases God and is heard by him?*

A. First, we must from the heart call upon the one true God only, who has revealed himself in his Word, for all that he has commanded us to pray. Second, we must thoroughly know our need and misery, so that we may humble ourselves before God. Third, we must rest on this firm foundation that, although we do not deserve it, God will certainly hear our prayer for the sake of Christ our Lord, as he has promised us in his Word.

In genuine prayer we approach (1) God alone, (2) without exalting anything in ourselves, and (3) only in the name of our Lord Jesus Christ.

1. We may direct our prayer exclusively to the One about whom the Bible, or Holy Scripture, speaks. This Scripture was given by God himself, first simply to Israel and now to descendants of Gentiles who through the preaching of the disciples have become Christians, worshipers of the heavenly Father.

2. We may direct our prayer exclusively to God in the awareness of our dependence on him. He is God, the Creator and Sustainer of all things, but we have been created by him and are sustained by him. In addition, through sin we have all become by nature unworthy creatures with respect to God.

3. We may approach God only in the name of our Lord Jesus Christ (John 16:23–24). Before Christ's coming it was from grace alone, but now only "for the sake of Christ" (see 2 Cor. 12:10; Phil. 1:29; 3:7; Phlm. 6).

Q&A 118

Q. *What has God commanded us to ask of him?*

A. All the things we need for body and soul, as included in the prayer which Christ our Lord himself taught us.

Spiritual and physical need includes what a person needs in every respect, in terms of both one's inner self and one's external needs. This involves knowing, loving, and serving God with our whole heart, as well as our protection from catastrophe, from lack, and from hunger, supplying all of this along with what a person needs for food and drink, clothing, shelter, and such, in order to stay alive.

Q&A 119

Q. *What is the Lord's Prayer?*

A. Our Father in heaven, hallowed be your name. Your kingdom come, your will be done, on earth as it is in heaven. Give us this day our daily bread, and forgive us our debts, as we also have forgiven our debtors. And lead us not into temptation, but deliver us from the evil one, for yours is the kingdom and the power and the glory forever. Amen.

In 1875 a document dating from the period shortly after the apostles (around A.D. 150) was discovered in a monastery in Constantinople. It is called "The Teaching of the Twelve Apostles" (*Didachē*). It contains the Lord's Prayer, among other things, and advises that people should pray this prayer three times each day.

The prayer speaks first of "your" and only then of "us." We begin with the things of God and then follow with our concerns.

Scripture References

Isaiah 42:8
> "I am the Lord; that is my name;
> my glory I give to no other,
> nor my praise to carved idols."

1 John 5:14
And this is the confidence that we have toward him, that if we ask anything according to his will he hears us.

LORD'S DAY 46

Q&A 120

Q. *Why has Christ commanded us to address God as our Father?*

A. To awaken in us at the very beginning of our prayer that childlike reverence and trust toward God which should be basic to our prayer: God has become our Father through Christ and will much less deny us what we ask of him in faith than our fathers would refuse us earthly things.

During the time of the Old Testament, people addressed the Lord as "Father" (Deut. 32:6; Isa 63:16; 64:8). What is striking is that the Lord Jesus commands us to begin our prayer saying *"Our* Father" or, just simply, "Father" (Luke 11:2). Jesus was seeking wisely to help us overcome our natural inclination as human beings to consider ourselves the most important. Let us remember that we are talking to God in fellowship with the universal Christian church throughout the ages. That is why we say, "Our Father."

With the address of the Lord's Prayer, Christ taught us two things, namely, reverence and trust.

Reverence first. Moses and Joshua had to remove their shoes in the presence of God (a custom in the ancient world of that day). We uncover our head. Isn't it extraordinary that we are addressing the King of kings?

Trust as well. Is it not also something extraordinary that this

Great King has given us and even our children in the cradle a multitude of promises? Promises for this life (food, drink, clothing) and for the life following our resurrection from the grave. We can address God confidently, heartily, and cordially as "our Father."

Q&A 121

Q. *Why is there added, in heaven?*

A. These words teach us not to think of God's heavenly majesty in an earthly manner, and to expect from his almighty power all things we need for body and soul.

By teaching us to address God as "our Father," Jesus taught us to be both reverent and trusting toward God. The additional phrase, "who is in heaven," serves, as it were, to underscore what was already said in the address.

Heaven itself (or we may also say, "the heavens") is the creation of his hand, together with the earth, which is occasionally called the footstool for God's feet, whereas heaven by contrast is his throne (Isa. 66:1).

Little wonder that the Preacher warns us, "Be not rash with your mouth, nor let your heart be hasty to utter a word before God, for God is in heaven and you are on earth. Therefore let your words be few" (Eccl. 5:2). No one has set any boundaries for God, and even the heavens cannot contain him (1 Kgs. 8:27).

Scripture References

Psalm 115:3
> Our God is in the heavens;
>> he does all that he pleases.

Romans 8:15
For you did not receive the spirit of slavery to fall back into fear, but you have received the Spirit of adoption as sons, by whom we cry, "Abba! Father!"

LORD'S DAY 47

Q. *What is the first petition?*

A. Hallowed be your name. That is: Grant us first of all that we may rightly know you, and sanctify, glorify, and praise you in all your works, in which shine forth your almighty power, wisdom, goodness, righteousness, mercy, and truth. Grant us also that we may so direct our whole life—our thoughts, words, and actions—that your name is not blasphemed because of us but always honored and praised.

Among civilized people, as soon as a baby is born, the child receives a name. Often the parents have decided long beforehand what that name will be. There are so many! Each of them is a sign for distinguishing the child among so many people!

But God is simply God, and for that reason he does not need such a name. When Scripture speaks about God's name, it is referring to something altogether different, namely, God's fame. God answered Moses's question about what his name was: I AM WHO I AM (Exod. 3:14). That became the Hebrew name of God. God would always be a helper near to his people. Just as with us, a mother answers her child who is calling for help, "Here I am! I'm right here, next to you!"

Jonah honestly informed the sailors of the ship who were caught in the storm that the tempest was caused not by the idol gods on whom they were calling for deliverance, but by Yahweh, the only true God who was worshiped in Israel (Jon. 1:5–17).

The Lord Jesus was referring to this God, with his unique name (or fame), when he taught his disciples the first petition. Near the conclusion of his stay on earth, he could say to his Father, "I glorified you on earth, having accomplished the work that you gave me to do. . . . I have manifested your name to the people whom you gave me out of the world" (John 17:4, 6). Scripture warns us to guard against God's name being blasphemed in the world as a result of our conduct (Isa. 52:5; Rom. 2:24).

Rather we must pray, "Father, *hallowed* be your name." That happened, for example, when the oldest two sons of Aaron, who were priests, brought strange fire before the face of the LORD and fire came forth from him that consumed them (Lev. 10:1–3). God himself could hallow his name, as we see from the lives of Moses (at Meribah, Num. 20:12; 27:14) and David (Bathsheba's first son; 2 Sam. 12:14). The point is that we are to ensure that we hallow God's name. So we frequently pray, "Teach me your way, O LORD, that I may walk in your truth; unite my heart to fear your name" (Ps. 86:11). To hallow God's name means to praise and glorify his name. If we Christians don't do that, who will?

Scripture References

Psalm 8:2

>Out of the mouth of babies and infants
>you have established strength because of your foes,
>>to still the enemy and the avenger.

Psalm 115:1–3

>Not to us, O LORD, not to us, but to your name give glory,
>>for the sake of your steadfast love and your faithfulness!
>Why should the nations say,
>>"Where is their God?"
>Our God is in the heavens;
>>he does all that he pleases.

LORD'S DAY 48

Q&A 123

Q. *What is the second petition?*

A. Your kingdom come. That is: So rule us by your Word and Spirit that more and more we submit to you. Preserve and increase your church. Destroy the works of the devil, every power that raises itself against you, and every conspiracy against your holy Word. Do all this until the fullness of your kingdom comes, wherein you shall be all in all.

The word *kingdom* can have more than one meaning, one of them being "a large territory." But because God has created everything, we can hardly pray that this already-existing territory come.

Here we can better understand the word *kingdom* to refer to kingship, rule, dominion, and we should not think simply in earthly terms. Jesus taught that his kingdom did not come with a display of military power. He would be riding on a donkey. He has comforted those who mourn in Zion. To his opponents, the Pharisees, he said, "The kingdom of God is in the midst of you" (Luke 17:21). Jesus, God's own Son, was standing before them here on earth. Therefore we may also say that God's kingdom has already come. Christ is already the Head of his church. He was that initially with the Jewish church. Thereafter the apostolic church brought the gospel of the kingdom everywhere (Acts 8:12; 14:22; 19:8; Col. 1:13).

In due course the kingdom of God will be perfected on earth, at the last day. Then the Scripture will be fulfilled by the *second* coming of Christ, this time in glory.

When we pray the second petition, "Your kingdom come," we are asking for two things: (1) that God's kingship may be acknowledged now in this world, and (2) that God will send our Savior to bring an end to all opposition. Daniel foretold precisely that (Dan. 2).

Scripture References

Matthew 6:33
"But seek first the kingdom of God and his righteousness, and all these things will be added to you."

1 John 3:8
Whoever makes a practice of sinning is of the devil, for the devil has been sinning from the beginning. The reason the Son of God appeared was to destroy the works of the devil.

LORD'S DAY 49

> ## Q&A 124
>
> **Q.** *What is the third petition?*
>
> **A.** Your will be done, on earth as it is in heaven. That is: Grant that we and all men may deny our own will, and without any murmuring obey your will, for it alone is good. Grant also that everyone may carry out the duties of his office and calling as willingly and faithfully as the angels in heaven.

We can speak of God's will in two ways. First, with reference to God's counsel, such as, for example, when God created heaven and earth, and he created human beings on earth in his image. We are not being taught to pray about God's will in that sense, since that has already occurred. But the word *will* can also mean "command" or "commandment." The Lord Jesus had that meaning in view when he taught his disciples the Lord's Prayer. That is clearly evident from the words Jesus added, "on earth as it is in heaven." Apparently he had in view the performance of God's commandments by the angels in heaven (Ps. 103:20–21).

If anyone may command us to pray that God's will be done, then surely it was our Savior. He gave us an unsurpassed example by doing everything that the Father had mandated for him. You can read a lot about this in the Old Testament prophets (e.g., Isa. 53). We read of the complete fulfillment of this in the Gospels (with regard to the cross and resurrection).

Scripture shows us the will of God for our daily practical living, when it speaks about his covenant with young and old, and commands us to put to death our old nature and to walk in new obedience. That is our sanctification.

Scripture References

Psalm 1:1–6

> Blessed is the man
> who walks not in the counsel of the wicked,
> nor stands in the way of sinners,
>   nor sits in the seat of scoffers;
> but his delight is in the law of the Lord,
>   and on his law he meditates day and night.
>
> He is like a tree
>   planted by streams of water
> that yields its fruit in its season,
>   and its leaf does not wither.
> In all that he does, he prospers.
> The wicked are not so,
>   but are like chaff that the wind drives away.
>
> Therefore the wicked will not stand in the judgment,
>   nor sinners in the congregation of the righteous;
> for the Lord knows the way of the righteous,
>   but the way of the wicked will perish.

Galatians 5:16–17

But I say, walk by the Spirit, and you will not gratify the desires of the flesh. For the desires of the flesh are against the Spirit, and the desires of the Spirit are against the flesh, for these are opposed to each other, to keep you from doing the things you want to do.

LORD'S DAY 50

Q&A 125

Q. *What is the fourth petition?*

A. Give us this day our daily bread. That is: Provide us with all our bodily needs so that we may acknowledge that you are the only fountain of all good, and that our care and labor, and also your gifts, cannot do us any good without your blessing. Grant, therefore, that we may withdraw our trust from all creatures and place it only in you.

We may assume that Adam and Eve acknowledged that all things came from God, including food, and everything they needed for daily life. But early people—today we simply call them pagans— lived on earth who bragged about their own strength and accomplishments, or made idols out of creatures like the sun, moon, and rain, all the while forgetting God our Creator and Sustainer.

Within Israel that knowledge of God was preserved when they sang about all creatures, "These all look to you, to give them their food in due season" (Ps. 104:27). Moses warned God's people that after some years had passed, they should not begin to think that their power and the strength of their hand had obtained for them all the blessings they enjoyed (Deut. 8). Moses commanded them to pray, "Look down from your holy habitation, from heaven, and bless your people Israel and the ground that you have given us" (Deut. 26:15).

The Lord Jesus spoke repeatedly about his Father as the Giver of all good gifts (Matt. 7:11; Luke 12:30). When he was being tempted, he resisted Satan with a citation from Deuteronomy 8: "It is written, 'Man shall not live by bread alone, but by every word that comes from the mouth of God'" (Matt. 4:4). And he commanded his disciples to pray to his heavenly Father, "Give us this day our daily bread" (Matt. 6:11).

Our Savior's lifestyle was far from wasteful—after multiplying the bread he had the leftover pieces (properly) gathered up—yet he told his disciples, "Do not be anxious about your life, what you will eat or what you will drink, nor about your body, what you will put on" (Matt. 6:25).

Someone might nonetheless ask, "How can we ask the Lord for bread when it is already prepared and ready on our table?"

We see the same thing when a child takes an apple from a bowl on the table, after first asking, "Mother, may I take an apple?" The child does this even though those apples were purchased for him. But Mother is the owner. In the same way, before we enjoy a finely furnished meal, we acknowledge our heavenly Father as the owner by saying, "Please."

We don't pray, "Give *me* my daily bread," but, "Give *us* our daily bread." We must not forget that we are praying to God, who through his covenant of grace is a Father who has many more children en route to the heavenly Canaan, the New Jerusalem, who also need food and drink.

Scripture References

Psalm 23:1–6
> The LORD is my shepherd; I shall not want.
>> He makes me lie down in green pastures.
> He leads me beside still waters.
>> He restores my soul.
> He leads me in paths of righteousness
>> for his name's sake.
>
> Even though I walk through the valley of the shadow of death,
>> I will fear no evil,

for you are with me;
>   your rod and your staff,
>   they comfort me.

You prepare a table before me in
>   the presence of my enemies;
you anoint my head with oil;
>   my cup overflows.
Surely goodness and mercy shall follow me
>   all the days of my life,
and I shall dwell in the house of the LORD
>   forever.

Psalm 145:16

You open your hand;
>   you satisfy the desire of every living thing.

Luke 12:15

And he said to them, "Take care, and be on your guard against all covetousness, for one's life does not consist in the abundance of his possessions."

LORD'S DAY 51

Our Lord Jesus was the only person on earth who never needed to pray for the forgiveness of sins. But his disciples do. Therefore, at their own request he taught them a prayer containing this petition.

Q&A 126

Q. *What is the fifth petition?*

A. Forgive us our debts, as we also have forgiven our debtors. That is: For the sake of Christ's blood, do not impute to us, wretched sinners, any of our transgressions, nor the evil which still clings to us, as we also find this evidence of your grace in us that we are fully determined wholeheartedly to forgive our neighbor.

Our Savior did not like bragging and showing off. It was never his goal to surround himself with a huge crowd of people. Nor was he interested in coming to the people primarily with something innovative. So the fifth petition of the Lord's Prayer was entirely in line with the ancient rule of the torah, that anyone coming to God with a sacrifice may not do so with any unresolved evil. Relevant to this was Proverbs 28:9: "If one turns away his ear from hearing the law, even his prayer is an abomination." Paul pointed to our obligation when we pray to raise "holy hands" (1 Tim. 2:8).

Here the Catechism calls us "wretched sinners." In so doing, it seeks not to accuse us but to remind us of our own confession that by nature we are inclined to hate God and our neighbor. Christ added to this petition these words: "as we forgive our debtors." According to Luke 11:4, actually what he said was, as I render it, "as we *have forgiven* our debtors," using the past tense in the original Greek. Once again this points to the ancient rule that God had instituted in the torah. This rule, which the torah stipulated for all prayers, was added by the Lord Jesus as an appendage to the prayer for forgiveness of sins. Notice how this petition requires a clear conscience!

Scripture References

Matthew 5:23–24
"So if you are offering your gift at the altar and there remember that your brother has something against you, leave your gift there before the altar and go. First be reconciled to your brother, and then come and offer your gift."

Luke 17:3
"Pay attention to yourselves! If your brother sins, rebuke him, and if he repents, forgive him."

LORD'S DAY 52

T he authors of the Catechism divided the rest of the Lord's Prayer into three subjects. That was wise, especially with a view to the sixth petition, which is not easy.

Q&A 127
Q. *What is the sixth petition?*
A. And lead us not into temptation, but deliver us from the evil one. That is: In ourselves we are so weak that we cannot stand even for a moment. Moreover, our sworn enemies— the devil, the world, and our own flesh—do not cease to attack us. Will you, therefore, uphold and strengthen us by the power of your Holy Spirit, so that in this spiritual war we may not go down to defeat, but always firmly resist our enemies, until we finally obtain the complete victory.

Let us begin by considering the meaning of the phrase "the evil one." With this phrase the Lord Jesus was referring to the devil, also called Satan and Beelzebul (Matt. 9:34; 12:24). In connection with these words, Satan is frequently called the tempter (see Mark 4:15; Luke 8:11–13). This word *tempt* appears also in Psalm 95:9, where God reminds Israel of the wilderness, "when your fathers put me to the test" (ESV)—or "tempted me" (see 1 Cor. 10:9; Heb. 3:8–9). In the episode of Jesus's temptation in the wilderness, Satan is mentioned in each of the accounts in Matthew, Mark, and Luke. Moses had in view this kind of tempting of God by humans when he said to his people, "You shall not put the LORD your God to the test, as you tested him at Massah" (Deut. 6:16).

When we pray the Lord's Prayer, we should think of being tempted by the devil.

God rules over all, we confessed in Lord's Day 9. But we also saw in that context that God's counsel is not implemented by people, angels, and devils as though they were "blocks and stones" (see Canons of Dort III/IV, art. 16) They remain responsible for their conduct.

In the sixth petition the Lord Jesus taught us to pray that God would not hand us over to our enemies—including not just people, but even the devil and his servants—on account of our sins. These enemies can exert such an influence on a person that Christ said to Peter, "Get behind me, Satan!" (Matt. 16:23; Mark 8:33)

With those three enemies of ours, the Catechism refers not only to Satan but also to the world and our own flesh. By the term *flesh* we understand pride, greed, covetousness, and the like. (see 1 John 2:15–17). The term *flesh* includes a reference to our own sinful nature as well. Therefore we should ask our heavenly Father especially that we might live pure and sober lives (1 Tim. 6:9). The term *world* can refer to the humanity that, judging by their conduct, refuses to have anything to do with God and his Word.

Q&A 128

Q. How do you conclude your prayer?

A. For yours is the kingdom and the power and the glory forever. That is: All this we ask of you because, as our King, having power over all things, you are both willing and able to give us all that is good, and because not we but your holy name should so receive all glory forever.

When reading Scripture, we repeatedly see that admirers of God's power and might are given to speaking his praise. After God's miracles against the Egyptians and in the wilderness, Moses sang (Exod. 15). David sings after his deliverance from Saul and the

Philistines (see 2 Sam. 22). God now gives us the opportunity to praise him. In this way he fulfills his covenant with Abraham.

Why do we exalt God's praise in the sixth petition? Because there is no one higher than God who is worthy of our praise.

For what purpose do we lift up all six petitions to God? Because he alone is our heavenly Father. The prayer that Jesus taught us begins very importantly with the address "Our Father."

Q&A 129

Q. *What does the word* Amen *mean?*

A. *Amen means: It is true and certain. For God has much more certainly heard my prayer than I feel in my heart that I desire this of him.*

When we read in Genesis 15:6 that Abraham believed the LORD (after receiving that promise that his descendants would be as numerous as the stars in the sky), we read literally that Abraham said *amen* to that promise of God. This means that he accepted that promise as something reliable and trustworthy. In the Hebrew language the word *'amen* can easily be turned into a verb—to *'amen* something—which comes out in English as "to believe something." This conclusion of the Catechism is humbly appropriate!

Scripture References

John 16:33:
"I have said these things to you, that in me you may have peace. In the world you will have tribulation. But take heart; I have overcome the world."

1 John 2:15–17
Do not love the world or the things in the world. If anyone loves the world, the love of the Father is not in him. For all that is in the world—the desires of the flesh and the desires of the eyes and pride of life—is not from the Father but is from the world. And the world is passing away along with its desires, but whoever does the will of God abides forever.

Contributors

Cornelis Vonk (1904–1993) was a Reformed preacher and pastor in the Netherlands during the middle third of the twentieth century. His sermons and studies are widely known and appreciated today as a warmly devotional and pastoral treatment of the Bible text.

Frans van Deursen is an emeritus Reformed preacher and pastor in the Netherlands. He has authored a number of commentaries in this series, on both Old and New Testament books. He continues to preach regularly and to contribute volumes for this series.

Nelson D. Kloosterman serves as executive director of Worldview Resources International and labors as the translator of the volumes in this series. He is an ordained minister (PCA) and lives in Indiana.

Jordan J. Ballor is a research fellow at the Acton Institute for the Study of Religion & Liberty and serves as executive editor of the *Journal of Markets & Morality*.

Made in the USA
Lexington, KY
31 December 2014